"Bishop Oliveto's story touches on one of today's deepest fault lines in church and society. Hers is a deeply personal, revealing memoir about love and unity in a denomination wrestling with division. In an engaging, even gripping, style, she brings the reader to the table where issues are no longer abstract but fully human. This book has the power to change hearts and minds."
— Jim Winkler, President and General Secretary, National Council of Churches

"Bishop Oliveto reveals a pastor's passion, theologian's rigor, servant's heart, pioneer's courage, and disciple's extraordinary capacity to articulate hard truths with clarity and love. This book is a blessing in multiple ways. It speaks to pastors, laity, leaders, and pilgrims on a faith journey with deeply moving stories and respect for persons of all persuasions."
— Jane Allen Middleton, retired Bishop, Northeastern Jurisdiction, The United Methodist Church

"If you are concerned with healing the many wounds of our spiritual and secular communities today, you will want to read this book. In writing that is at once authentic and powerful, Bishop Oliveto challenges every one of us to do the hard—and yet deeply rewarding—work of building community, especially with those whom we see as 'the other.'"
— Bernard Schlager, Executive Director, Center for LGBTQ and Gender Studies in Religion, Pacific School of Religion

"I encourage people who are unable to accept LGBTQ persons in the leadership of the church, such as my colleague Bishop Karen Oliveto, to read her story. As she says, all of

D1604040

us—including her—need to scale an empathy wall because there is always someone we are 'othering.' Her story and reflections help us put on our climbing gear!"

— Sally Dyck, Bishop, Northern Illinois Conference, The United Methodist Church

"In disarming personal stories and profound biblical reflections, Bishop Oliveto invites us to encounter one another at the table across a divide that is threatening our ability to bear witness to a world in need. She challenges us to imagine 'How do we tell our own truth, while not denying the truth of another?' In the rich Christian tradition of personal witness, Bishop Oliveto beautifully weaves her story and the church's story in a way that embodies an invitation to grace."

— David Vasquez-Levy, President, Pacific School of Religion

"Karen Oliveto's story of faith, compassion, and love gathers us with our great diversity to meet one another face-to-face over a sacred meal. Her clarity and commitment to stay and welcome all to the table give us hope amid profound angst, fracture, and violence in our faith communities, country, and global village. Her faith is undergirded by Christ's welcome to break through unjust policies and oppressive systems that label anyone as 'less than' or participate in making anyone 'the other.' As pastor, preacher, prophet, and bishop, she lives into and means all are welcome and all are invited equally."

— Janie Adams Spahr, Honorably Retired Presbyterian lesbian minister and former minister director of That All May Freely Serve

# TOGETHER
# AT THE TABLE

# TOGETHER AT THE TABLE

*Diversity without Division in The United Methodist Church*

KAREN P. OLIVETO

WESTMINSTER
JOHN KNOX PRESS
LOUISVILLE • KENTUCKY

*First edition*
Published by Westminster John Knox Press
Louisville, Kentucky

18 19 20 21 22 23 24 25 26 27—10 9 8 7 6 5 4 3 2 1

Unless otherwise indicated, Scripture quotations are from the New Revised Standard Version of the Bible, copyright © 1989 by the Division of Christian Education of the National Council of the Churches of Christ in the U.S.A., and are used by permission.

Scripture quotations marked CEB are from the *Common English Bible*, © 2011 Common English Bible.

Excerpt from "Come to the Table of Grace," by Barbara Hamm, © 2008 Hope Publishing Company, Carol Stream, IL 60188. All rights reserved. Used by permission.

*Book design by Drew Stevens*
*Cover design by designpointinc.com*
*Cover photo by Alain McLaughlin*

**Library of Congress Cataloging-in-Publication Data**

Names: Oliveto, Karen P., 1958- author.
Title: Together at the table : diversity without division in the United Methodist Church / Karen P. Oliveto.
Description: Louisville, KY : Westminster John Knox Press, 2018. | Includes bibliographical references. |
Identifiers: LCCN 2018007902 (print) | LCCN 2018020808 (ebook) | ISBN 9781611648881 (ebk.) | ISBN 9780664263607 (pbk. : alk. paper)
Subjects: LCSH: Homosexuality--Religious aspects--United Methodist Church (U.S.) | Ordination of gays--United Methodist Church (U.S.) | Oliveto, Karen P., 1958- | United Methodist Church (U.S.)--Doctrines.
Classification: LCC BX8385.H65 (ebook) | LCC BX8385.H65 O455 2018 (print) | DDC 261.8/357660882876--dc23
LC record available at https://lccn.loc.gov/2018007902

Most Westminster John Knox Press books are available at special quantity discounts when purchased in bulk by corporations, organizations, and special-interest groups. For more information, please e-mail SpecialSales@wjkbooks.com.

*To Nellie Oliveto*
*—my Mum—*
*for always making sure there was room*
*for one more at the table.*

# CONTENTS

# ACKNOWLEDGMENTS

Writing may seem like a solitary endeavor, but that is far from the truth. Every part of the creation of this book highlighted, for me, how interconnected we are. Even when sitting in my study to write behind a closed door, I was aware that surrounding me was a great cloud of witnesses—people from my past, present, and, yes, even future—who helped form my thinking and therefore my life.

I want to thank Westminster John Knox Press for reaching out to me in what seemed like hours after my election, inviting me to write for them. At that time, my life had been turned upside down, and I told them to ask me again in about four months. Almost to the day, they got back in touch with me, and this book had its beginning. I am grateful to my editor, Jessica Miller Kelley, who pushed at the right times and places to make my writing clearer. She is a great coach and midwife!

Throughout my ministry, I have been blessed with amazing colleagues and companions. I am particularly grateful for those I work side by side with in the Mountain Sky Area of The United Methodist Church, as we seek to put into practice much of this book as we live into Beloved Community together.

The family kitchen table that kept expanding to include not only my immediate family but also aunts, uncles, cousins, nieces, nephews, and people we loved (or were learning to love) was a place where relational wisdom was passed on. For those who prepared the meals and those who were guests at the table, I thank you for the ways you continue to nourish my body and my soul.

Lastly, I am grateful to my spouse, Robin Ridenour, who patiently put up with writing sessions that bookended my work days and started many mornings of vacation for the past year. Your encouragement sustains me, your generosity inspires me, and your love gives me deep joy.

# INTRODUCTION

Dinner was always a sacred time in my family. My parents divorced when I was young. This was before the term "single-parent family" was commonly used. Instead, my sisters and I were defined as coming from a "broken home." But there was one time when this broken family was made whole—at the dinner table. My mother made sure that her work shifts allowed her to be home for dinner. As the mealtime approached, she would call out through the neighborhood, "Ka-Al-La"—blending our names (Karen, Alison, Lauren) together—calling us away from whatever games we were playing with friends. But she never called us away from our friends. Whoever was playing with us was invited to our table as well. Our table of four often held six, eight, even twelve, causing one of my mom's friends who stopped by during a meal to pull my mother aside and whisper: "Are you running some kind of group home here?"

Any playground fights were forgotten as we passed the pasta. Sibling squabbles fell away at the dinner table. At the table, we shared our day, our accomplishments in school, and those things that troubled us. We might not have crossed each other's paths during the day, but at the dinner table, our broken family became whole.

Perhaps this is why I value Communion so much. This Christian ritual, which remembers Jesus' last meal with his disciples, is a sacrament of belonging. At Christ's Table, new kinship lines are drawn. In the act of giving and receiving the bread and cup, it is not only broken lives that are restored, but broken relationships as well. We become connected in deeper ways not only with those who surround the table with us, but with all those, in all times and places, who have approached Christ's Table with hands outstretched.

From an early age, Communion has mattered to me. I recall the first time I received Communion at my home church, Babylon United Methodist Church on Long Island, when I was confirmed. The power of that moment kneeling at the altar rail with church friends I had known since I first stepped foot in a musty church basement for Sunday school at the age of four remains one of the most profound moments of my life. I was aware that the act was not a solitary one, but one I shared with these long-time friends. In the years to come, as we entered high school, we shared Communion regularly together during youth group meetings and on retreats. And every first Sunday of the month, we stepped down from the choir loft to kneel again at the altar rail, to once again share in this sacred meal.

Things were not always rosy with us. As it is with most high schoolers, we had our quarrels, resentments, and cliques. But, in contrast to what I experienced in my high school, conflicts in our youth group were not insurmountable and never caused us to break relationship with each other. The main difference between my experience in church and high school was Communion. The meal really does have power.

I remember one humid summer night, shortly before several of us were heading off to college, when we decided to go crabbing in the Great South Bay. Two friends had boats, and we piled into them. There was the usual joking and jabbing. But as we cut the engines in the middle of the bay, silence descended as we took our positions on the boats. On each, one person steered, two people stood on either side with flashlights, seeking to spot blue-claw crabs, while two people stood near them with nets, ready to ensnare the highlighted crustaceans. We were seamless as we worked effortlessly together. The years of shared church-going activities had imprinted deep within us a way to live and work together. After each boat had a bushel of crabs, we returned to the shore, where we shared a communion of crabs and Coca-Cola. We were aware that even though this might be the last night we would ever be together, we were intimately entwined with one another.

It was in the Beloved Community found at Babylon United Methodist Church that I heard my call to ordained ministry. Even as a young child, sitting in a Sunday school room filled with flannel board cutouts of people from the Bible, I knew I had found a home. The Bible, filled with stories of ordinary women and men doing shocking and extraordinary things, became a road map for me as I grew deeper in love with God and the church. Their story was my story—it's the story of all of us who seek a connection with a God who longs for us as much as we long for God.

The Babylon church was extremely committed to its children and youth. As a fourth grader, I attended the Wesley Choir, one of the church's five choirs (only the Chancel Choir was for adults the rest were all for the young people of the church). The very first hymn I learned in the choir was "I Sing the Almighty Power of God" by Isaac Watts:

> I sing th' almighty power of God,
> that made the mountains rise,
> That spread the flowing seas abroad,
> and built the lofty skies.

I sing the wisdom that ordained
the sun to rule the day;
The moon shines full at God's command,
and all the stars obey.

I sing the goodness of the Lord,
who filled the earth with food,
Who formed the creatures thru the Word,
and then pronounced them good.
Lord, how Thy wonders are displayed,
where'er I turn my eye,
If I survey the ground I tread,
or gaze upon the sky.

There's not a plant or flower below,
but makes thy glories known,
And clouds arise, and tempests blow,
by order from thy throne;
While all that borrows life from thee
is ever in thy care;
And everywhere that we can be,
thou, God art present there.[1]

Reading over these lines now makes me realize how deep
they dwell within my soul. Since early childhood, God has
been a constant companion. In every step I have taken,
whether high on a mountain pass or on a gritty city street,
the power and presence of God has revealed itself in beauty
and unexpected moments of grace. Sometimes, this has
caused such a profound ache within my heart that I have
had to stop in my tracks to fully take in this awareness.

Just as John and Charles Wesley intended, the
choir songs and church hymns added to the Sunday

school lessons and transmitted faith deep within me. Singing became an embodied way to grasp the mystery of God and the ways of Jesus. My choir director, the Rev. Ken White, engaged and delighted all of us who sang under his tutelage, and he imparted a joy that comes with the Christian faith that has undergirded my life ever since.

I found myself drawn deeper and deeper into the life of the church, even while still in elementary school. Who could resist a place where the unconditional love and acceptance of God was lived out so fully? I thrived in that community. One day when I was eleven years old, while standing in the church kitchen, Ken turned to me and asked, "What do you want to be when you grow up?" "An astronomer," I replied.

It was true, and it was all because of my Sunday school class. In second grade, we learned about the power of stories to shape how people lived. Some of the lessons included Roman and Greek myths, and we learned of Orion, the hunter who Zeus placed in the stars. I was fascinated by the tale, and wanted to learn more, so I went to the public library. (Even then I had a library card. To this day, whenever I move, registering for a library card takes priority over the car registration and getting a new driver's license.) There was just one problem: I was in second grade and didn't understand that the culture bound stories behind constellations would be in a section on mythology and not a section on astronomy. Knowing that Orion was a constellation, I headed to the astronomy section. I never found that myth spelled out like it had been in Sunday school, but I did fall in love with the night sky, filled with stars and planets and unseen worlds.

Perhaps "unseen" is the operative word here.

A couple of years later, a teacher noted my difficulty in reading the chalkboard and had my mother take me to an optometrist. I had very bad eyesight all through my childhood, so as much as I was in love with the night sky, I couldn't see much of it! Even though I couldn't make out the constellations, that didn't make me love astronomy any less.

Until Ken's question broke open my world.

He responded to my answer with another question: "Did you ever think about becoming a minister?" There was an electricity that flowed through my body with his question. Even though I had never seen a woman minister, his question helped all the pieces of my life come together. I knew from that moment on what God had created me to do and began to prepare for a life of service through ordained ministry.

This call was affirmed over and over again, both within the Babylon UMC community and beyond, as I entered college. God continued to be a very real presence in my life, particularly through music and community. In seminary, however, God suddenly disappeared from my life and I felt myself wandering in the wilderness, a soul in exile. As with most seminarians, my first year of study deconstructed my faith and life. In the brokenness, I had to face parts of myself that I had tried hard to suppress my entire life. I listened to the stories of gay and lesbian students and recognized myself in their stories. I struggled deeply, realizing that for most of my life I knew there was something different about me, even before I had a name for it.

I wrestled with this for a full year. When I finally stopped fighting and just embraced who I was, I experienced the miracle of the "peace which passes all understanding" descend upon my heart. As the pieces of my life finally fit and God returned, I learned an important lesson:

God doesn't ever leave us. We leave God when we deny who we are and who God created us to be.

There was one other time early in my ministry when I had a crisis of faith, wondering, was this Jesus story really true, or was I offering a myth to those in my care? What if it was made up? What if there really was no God? I am not sure what precipitated this loss of faith, but I remember it as truly a dark night of the soul.

As one who was getting paid to talk about God and to invite people into a relationship with the Divine, this was not only an existential crisis but an ethical one as well. How could I get up on Sunday morning and preach about something I was no longer sure about? John Wesley's words helped me through this wilderness wandering: "Preach faith till you have it."[2] That helped me "go through the motions." But what helped restore my faith—even deepen it—was Communion. As I stood before my rural congregation in upstate New York, the Communion ritual broke me open. The words of the liturgy not only spoke of an ancient truth but also of one I had experienced in my own life. As I saw hands outstretched to reach for the bread I offered, I saw the eyes of each person, full of longing, despair, heartache, yet also, hope. The power of Communion to heal and unite reminded me of my early Communion experiences. I recalled the ways the meal mended broken hearts and broken relationships. The Christ who is present in the meal unites us in deep and profound ways, across our differences and disagreements, and helps our fractured selves become whole.

Communion restored my faith and brought me home to Beloved Community.

In July 2016, I was elected by the delegates of the Western Jurisdiction of The United Methodist Church to the episcopacy. I am the first openly LGBTQ person to serve as bishop in the global denomination. My election has highlighted tensions within the denomination. For decades, there has been a growing theological and cultural divide in the church, particularly as the denomination grows exponentially outside the United States. The issue of homosexuality has visibly revealed the fault line of division within the church.

Some people have regarded my election as healing balm. After decades of "second-class status" in the church, LGBTQ persons and their families finally felt that the church could include them. The grace they had experienced in their own lives was now lived out in the church. Others have regarded my election as a sign of a church that is falling apart, straying from essential tenets of faith and breaking church law. The United Methodist Church is feeling more and more like the typo I often make: "Untied." The Table of Grace, where we encounter Christ and each other, has become a table of suspicion: Who can sit at the table and join in the meal? Only those who think like us, or everyone? My election has helped some claim the Table, while causing others to opt out of the feast.

At the same time, the world feels increasingly fractured. In spite of social media, which is shrinking the global village by bringing far-off cultures into our homes via laptops and smartphones, our divisions seem highlighted, mocking any understanding of our common humanity and residence on the same planet. The fear of the other has become heightened. As a result, communities and nations are figuratively and literally erecting walls to keep people out.

Perhaps it is my old love of astronomy that draws me to the biographies of astronauts. More than the question of what the "right stuff" was that had them rise to the top and be chosen to leave our gravitational pull, I was more interested in what they saw and experienced in space:

> I really believe that if the political leaders of the world could see their planet from a distance of 100,000 miles their outlook could be fundamentally changed. That all-important border would be invisible, that noisy argument silenced. The tiny globe would continue to turn, serenely ignoring its subdivisions, presenting a unified facade that would cry out for unified understanding, for homogeneous treatment. The earth must become as it appears: blue and white, not capitalist or Communist; blue and white, not rich or poor; blue and white, not envious or envied.
> — Michael Collins, Gemini 10 and Apollo 11 astronaut[3]

> The first day or so we all pointed to our countries. The third or fourth day we were pointing to our continents. By the fifth day, we were aware of only one Earth.
> — Sultan bin Salman Al-Saud, space shuttle payload specialist[4]

> When you're finally up at the moon looking back on earth, all those differences and nationalistic traits are pretty well going to blend, and you're going to get a concept that maybe this really is one world and why the hell can't we learn to live together like decent people.
> — Frank Borman, Apollo 8 astronaut[5]

The view from space gave the astronauts a new perspective on earth. Borders faded and what emerged was humanity's shared life together on this small, spinning orb. One does not need to take a trip to outer space to gain this perspective. This is the essence of every faith tradition. Strangers become kin we didn't know we had. Divisions of class, culture, and language fall away as we discover the Divine: all of life is sacred—every being is sacred because each possesses the mark of the Creator. This connects us in deep ways.

When I approach the altar rail for Communion, it can feel like the most solitary journey I have ever taken. Yet when I reach for the bread and cup, and then rise from the table, my perspective has changed. Like those astronauts from space, I have a new view: I arise more deeply aware of my oneness with those around me.

We need to understand and embrace our connectedness now more than ever before. We need to restore our relationship with the earth, with all living creatures, with one another. We cannot erect walls to keep us separate. This separation creates a sense that there are those "not like us," which can lead to exploitation, oppression, and injustice. Yet, even religious traditions compete with each other, and adherents of one faith deny the faithfulness found in another's faith tradition. Holy wars continue to be fought over "truth" and "right." One's sacred rituals are not honored by another, but are held in suspect, lacking any sense that these, too, can be a pathway to connection with the Divine.

At a time when communities, churches, and society are divided by competing theologies and ideologies, what is missing in our conversations with each other, particularly with those who hold beliefs different from our own? How do we stand before one another and relearn the art of conversation through empathy? How do we tell our own truth, while not denying the truth of another?

The inspiration for these questions, and, in the pages to come, my responses to them, have come out of a time of great trial for me as I seek to understand those who are angry with my election to the episcopacy. The questions are for *me*: How can I maintain relationship with those who disagree with me, not only with what I believe but with who I am? What does unity look like in the face of disagreement? Can we speak not *at* each other, but *with* each other? Can I dare to be vulnerable in the face of anger and distrust? What can lead us all to a different place?

My hope and prayers are that this book might provide some insight into the way forward, so that what is "untied" will be woven into a new unity, and fractured relationships will give way to Beloved Community.

This book would not be possible without the love and support of my most intimate conversation partner, my spouse, Robin Ridenour. Her patience, wisdom, and compassion help me be a better me. It is the faith we share, embodied in our living, that has been the source of the insights found in these pages.

When I was serving as senior pastor of Glide Memorial Church in San Francisco, Saturday nights would find us pouring over cookbooks, considering a new recipe to try. After church the next day, we'd pick up groceries and spend the rest of the afternoon in the kitchen, cooking. Friends would stop by as evening approached, and our dining room table would remind me of my mom's table when I was a child. We never knew who would join us for dinner, but by the time the meal was finished cooking, the table would be filled. Our godson, Liam, and his parents, visitors from out of town, church folks, activist friends, straight and queer people, all would break bread together. Sometimes our friends brought their friends. As at the Communion table that morning, all were welcomed at our dinner table. It didn't matter whether or not we knew our tablemates well, or even liked them at first. The conversation would be lively, filled with laughter as well as debate, as we each revealed more of who we were to each other. And this truth never failed to be revealed: *We eat with people we love.*

Chapter 1

# THE FRACTURED
# FAMILY TABLE

The lessons of my early childhood taught me that fights
never last long, and someone who might be on an opposing
team one day might be your most valuable player the next.
Growing up on the South Shore of Long Island, my sisters and friends were rarely found in our homes. Typical of
the burgeoning growth of suburbia post–World War II, we
lived on a dead-end block of identical houses. Our parents
were first-time homeowners, having moved out onto the
island from the city, thanks to generous GI bills. As a result,
the kids on our block were all close in age and, except for
those who were enrolled in parochial school, went through
elementary and secondary education together.

Whether the days were lazy and humid or blustery
and snowy, we were out in the streets once we finished our
morning chores. Summers meant building forts made out of
sheets tied to the chain-link fences that separated our proper-
ties, endless games of softball in the streets, running through
sprinklers, climbing trees, or hopping fences as dusk fell and
the nightly game of hide and seek began, or, on rainy days,
playing games of Monopoly that never seemed to end. Winter meant tag football, skating on ponds, snowball fights, and
running fiercely down the icy street to belly flop on our sleds,
which was, on the flat South Shore, the only way we could
gain momentum enough to enjoy sledding.

We did fight with each other, but it never lasted very long. Given the games we played and the number of kids on the block, we would need each other if we wanted to continue to play those games. So, we didn't so much "make up" after quarrels, hashing out who was wrong and who was right; we really did simply "forgive and forget" so the game could continue. Even at that age, we realized that alliances—like the teams we choose—shift. One is never right all the time, nor is one wrong all the time. Recognizing this helped us keep ourselves focused on what really mattered to us: playing our games. It helped us work through our fights and disagreements quickly.

I watch our nieces and nephews as they grow up. Spontaneous play seems to be a lost art. Instead, play dates for the younger ones are arranged and carefully scheduled by parents, and any squabbles over toys are quickly resolved by the hovering grown-ups. The older ones amuse themselves with video games, often playing against avatars of people whose real names they will never know.

What happens when winning and losing become more important than building a team and maintaining morale? What kind of adults are we shaping, who no longer know how to work through problems together? When ending friendships becomes a simple click of an "unfriend" button on social media, or deleting someone's avatar, are we helping young people have the emotional resiliency to focus on building and maintaining relationships, even when there is disagreement?

Changes in play are not the only thing I am noticing about life in the early twenty-first century: We no longer know how to sit at the table together. Studies show that only 28 percent of families eat together at home seven days a week.[1] At one time, the dining room table was the reconnecting point for families. After a day of work, school, or play, it was the time when the stresses and grievances of the day could be aired and released. Studies show that dining together regularly can create healthy lives. A study by the National Center on Addiction and Substance Abuse (CASA) at Columbia University found in 2003 that teenagers who eat with their families only once or twice a week (or not at all) are "twice as likely to take drugs, more likely to be 'high stress,' more likely to say they are often bored, and less likely to perform well in school than teens who eat with their families 5 to 7 times a week."[2]

As families have fewer meals together, the number of people eating alone has risen dramatically in the past few decades. There was a time when eating alone was an anomaly. There was a social awkwardness to sitting at a restaurant as the sole diner. Now, half of all meals are eaten alone.[3] What happens to a civilization that no longer shares meals together? What breaks down in a culture when a once-social (and necessary) aspect of living in community is no longer the norm? What part of our common humanity is lost when we fail to stop and break bread together?

We live in a time of unprecedented access to one another. Social media enables us to see world events as they happen, not just during a 6 p.m. news broadcast. In spite of a shrinking global village, which has been made possible through technology, there is an increasing provincialism and tightening of borders and boundaries. During the US presidential election of 2016, we heard, "Build a wall!" as the rallying cry of one of the candidates. In June of that same year, voters in the United Kingdom passed a referendum to have their country leave the European Union. Polls showed that a desire to stem the immigration flow to Britain was a driving force for Brexit.

Deep divisions are causing a rising tide of intolerance, bullying, and violence. The behavior modeled by many national leaders, including President Donald Trump, has created space for white supremacists to be more vocal in their hate speech[4] and has offered tacit approval of bullying behavior.[5] Teachers are reporting a sharp rise in bullying behavior in schools. Social media is often used as a platform for bullying. A study by the Cyberbullying Research Center found that 34 percent of young people in 2016 had been bullied online.[6] There is a growing lack of civility in discourse that is creating chasms in place of community.

When I was a youngster, church was the place where I was free from bullying. In school, taunts were frequent, but church was a sanctuary—not just for me but for many of my peers. At a recent reunion of my high school youth group, fifty of us came home to Babylon UMC for a weekend. We headed to the beach, sitting on the sand and catching up on each other's lives. One person said something that we all knew to be true: "We were all odd kids, but at church, we found acceptance."

It was through the foundation of faith given to me by the Sunday school teachers, youth group leaders, music ministers, and pastors that I experienced God's unconditional love and unconditional acceptance. This grace was experienced over and over again, not only through affirmation of what I did well, but also poured out in forgiveness when I erred. The community of faith nurtured me in ways that allowed me to explore who I was and who I was called to be. It didn't matter that I was a bit of a "nerd." Here, I was encouraged to be the best nerd I could be, which meant to live fully into who God created me to be, learning from my mistakes, and moving joyfully forward.

I was in the Wesley Choir when I was in elementary school. Ken White, our music minister, had once invited me to bring my guitar to choir rehearsal and play with the choir. What Ken hadn't bargained for was that in my young mind, that meant he wanted me to bring it *every* week. Without skipping a beat, Ken made sure there was a song I could play along to in nearly every rehearsal. While I was in junior high, the church made a record album with Christmas and Easter music of our five choirs. Ken had me play guitar on one of the songs. I wince whenever I listen to the song, because I can now hear every missed note and wrong rhythm. Over the years, this has provided an important lesson for me, one that I need reminding of regularly: we don't need to be perfect in what we do, but we need to earnestly bring our best to it. Ken included me in the record, even though I would now question whether my guitar playing was worthy of being recorded for posterity. In this experience, I learned something of God's extravagant grace. This was what the church offered all my friends and me: a place where we were showered with love, affection, and encouragement. In this way, we all came to know ourselves loved by the God who created us and continually envelops us in grace.

It was with this undergirding of love and acceptance that I began to live into my call as an ordained minister in The United Methodist Church. When I heard my call to ordained ministry in 1969, this church was newly formed from a 1968 merger between The Methodist Church and the Evangelical United Brethren Church. At the time, I was not yet aware of my sexual orientation, nor did the UMC have any official policy regarding LGBTQ people in ordained ministry.

## AN UNTIED CHURCH

The history of The United Methodist Church includes many fissures and fractures. It is a story, when told from the vantage point of the margins, of exclusion based tenuously on Scripture or for political expediency. In 1787, Methodist minister Richard Allen walked out of a Philadelphia church because of discrimination: As the numbers of blacks increased in the Philadelphia church, a balcony was made for them to sit in. Blacks were forcibly removed from the lower floor, even in the midst of prayer. Additionally, black Methodist preachers were only allowed in the pulpits of all-black churches. In response, Allen founded the African Methodist Episcopal Church, a place where blacks could foster their spiritual development, respond to God's call, and grow in Christian commitment free from white racism.

This reach of racism became heightened over the issue of slavery by the mid-1800s. Even though John Wesley, the founder of Methodism, spoke out against the evils of slavery, saying, "Liberty is the right of every human creature, as soon as he breathes the vital air. And no human law can deprive him of that right, which derives from the law of nature," this commitment by Methodists eroded, stirring much debate between the northern and southern parts of the church over whether a person could own slaves.[7] After a lengthy, six-week General Conference in 1844, the Methodist Episcopal Church experienced a schism as southern Methodists formed the Methodist Episcopal Church, South (MECS).

Within the MECS were more than 207,000 black members, people who had been converted to Methodism while slaves. In 1866, after abolition left only 78,000 black members, the MECS General Conference asked, "What shall be done to promote the religious interests of the colored people?" It was decided that the "best interests" would be for black Methodists to have their own church, and in 1870 the Colored Methodist Episcopal Church was formed.[8]

The Methodist Episcopal Church and the Methodist Episcopal Church, South, reunified in 1939, but at the expense of blacks: a segregated jurisdiction was created solely for black churches so that racial prejudice by the southern churches could continue unchecked and unchallenged.

"The Central Jurisdiction was a compromise," said William McClain, a professor at Wesley Theological Seminary in Washington, D.C., who was ordained in the Central Alabama Conference in the Central Jurisdiction. "It was a way that the church avoided integration. It was a compromise to bring the southern Methodist Church and the northern Methodist Church together and to merge them in 1939. The truth was that black people were abused, insulted and disappointed that the church was not willing to be one church."[9]

Women in the church also faced marginalization. While John Wesley issued a license to preach to a woman in 1761, it would take nearly two hundred years for women to receive the right to full ordination. This occurred in 1956, just two years before my birth. In 1880, Anna Howard Shaw became the first woman to be ordained in the Methodist Protestant Church, but she was not granted full clergy rights.

Shaw heard the call to ministry when she was a young girl and did not let scriptural norms, Christian tradition, or the confines of her culture deter her from living out this call. With humor and a commitment to bearing witness to God's power, she entered seminary and endured much hardship and prejudice from her fellow students and churchmen. Her male classmates constantly taunted her, relying on what they perceived as scriptural norms to attempt to keep her in her place.

One classmate asked her, "Sister Shaw, why do you wear your hair short, when other women wear their hair long?"

Sensing that she was being set up, Shaw replied, "I see that you ask this sincerely, so I will tell you: it is a birthmark, I was born with short hair."

During one ordination interview, she was asked what she would do if her husband should refuse to allow her to preach, since Paul said that wives must obey their husbands. She replied that "Paul did not say so, according to the Scriptures. But even if he did, it would not concern me, for I am a spinster." The other minister countered, saying that she might marry someday.

"Possibly . . . wiser women than I am have married. But it is equally possible that I might marry a man who would command me to preach; and in that case I want to be all ready to obey him."[10] Shaw never married, but she was partnered. She lived her life with Susan B. Anthony's niece, Lucy. Their home in Cape Cod, a gathering place for activist women, was known as "Shaw's Adam-less Eden."

Women and people of color continue to face marginalization within The United Methodist Church. Clergy in The United Methodist Church serve under appointment, a system of deploying pastors by the bishop rather than hiring by the local church. Even under such a system, women and people of color earn less than their white male colleagues. They also serve smaller churches. When I became senior pastor of Glide Memorial Church in San Francisco, a church of 11,000 members, I broke the stained glass ceiling by becoming the first woman to serve in any of the denomination's top 100 largest churches. Sadly, eight years later when I was elected to the episcopacy, I was still the only woman on that list.

In 1972, the newly formed United Methodist Church addressed homosexuality. The church was developing a set of statements called the Social Principles to direct its prophetic and pastoral witness. Noting the emergence of the gay liberation movement as a result of the Stonewall riots in New York City in 1969, when LGBTQ patrons of a gay bar fought back against a police raid, those creating the Social Principles knew they needed to address the issue. In 1972, this paragraph was presented to the delegates of the General Conference[11] of the UMC:

> Homosexual persons, no less than heterosexual persons, are persons of sacred worth, who need the ministry and guidance of the church in their struggles for human fulfillment, as well as the spiritual and emotional care of a fellowship which enables reconciling relationships with God, with others and with self. Further, we insist that all persons are entitled to have their human and civil rights ensured.

This statement, which neither condemned nor condoned homosexuality, offered a pastoral instruction for the church to engage its LGBTQ members. However, when the paragraph was brought to the floor of General Conference, a bitter debate ensued. Before the paragraph was accepted, an amendment was approved which replaced the period at the end of the last sentence with a comma and then added the line: "though we do not condone the practice of homosexuality and consider this practice incompatible with Christian teaching." While there was no clarity on what constituted homosexual "practice" or on what Christian teaching this was based on, a purely pastoral statement became one of condemnation. Since that time, all future anti-LGBTQ policies would evolve from this statement, including an official policy that "self-avowed practicing homosexuals" may not be ordained.

But when I had my call to ordained ministry, there was no such policy. I knew I was a child of God, steeped in Wesleyan spirituality, and called to serve The United Methodist Church. This call was recognized and affirmed by communities of faith again and again. My meetings with district and conference boards of ordained ministries were always encouraging. My dismay and despair were great when I came out as a lesbian in seminary and realized—for the first time—that the church's welcome of me and my gifts was conditional.

This felt like a major bait and switch: the church that had nurtured me in the faith, helped me understand that I was a beloved child of God, and encouraged me to pursue ministry now added new conditions that suddenly invalidated all of it. What would I do? Where would I serve?

## COMING OUT AND INTO GOD'S GRACE

God's call to me, to serve in The United Methodist Church, was clear. My spirituality, steeped in the Wesleyan spirituality of personal piety and social holiness, had a home in the UMC that no other denomination could provide. The church that had cradled me from the infancy of my Christian journey turned out to have a cruel streak. As a pastor in San Francisco, I would minister to many LGBTQ youth and young adults whose parents had kicked them out of their homes when they discovered their child's sexual orientation. The church had become that parent for me and many LGBTQ people who experienced God's generous grace in the pews of the church, but now found pulpits that were closed to us and faced expulsion if we heard a call to ordained ministry.

But God is greater than our human institutions. I had tried to look at joining other, LGBTQ-welcoming denominations (which at the time included the United Church of Christ, the Unitarian Universalists, the Metropolitan Community Church, or The United Church of Canada), but it was to The United Methodist Church that I was called. God made a way for me—and for many others—when it seemed there was no way. Church leaders, congregants, boards of ministries, district superintendents, and bishops continued to nurture and affirm my call to ordained ministry.

People have accused me of lying about my sexual orientation, saying that since the church's stance is clear, I should not have pursued ordination. There is so much that is flawed in that statement, and it demonstrates how the church fosters a lack of understanding regarding human sexuality and seeks to constrain the movement of the Holy Spirit. It also reveals our inability to trust the truth of another's experience.

What does it mean to "practice" my sexual orientation? My sexual orientation is a lens through which I encounter and love the world, God, and human beings. The particularity of our personhood—our gender, skin color, religion, and so many other things—gives us each our own lens. I could not any more stop "practicing" who God created me to be than to voluntarily stop breathing.

It is an innate part of me. It is how I move in the world. I have never tried to "pass" as straight. I have never denied my sexual orientation. When I walked into rooms to be examined by boards of ordained ministry, I walked in as my authentic self. These boards saw and affirmed that call, not because I was perceived to be straight, but because I was received as a child of God who was called and equipped by God to serve the church.

I came out—as many clergy do—in seminary, for there is a deep connection between one's sexuality and one's spirituality. Both hit at the heart of one's being. The seminary experience is one of deconstruction. All the previously held understandings of one's faith—Scripture, the nature of God, who Jesus is—are challenged in ways that shake the very foundations of one's life. In this breaking and subsequent rebuilding, long-suppressed suspicions about my sexuality came to the surface. While God had been a very real and active presence in my life prior to seminary, God suddenly disappeared, and I felt myself wandering in the wilderness, a soul in exile. I listened to the stories of gay and lesbian students and recognized myself in their stories. I struggled deeply, realizing that for most of my life I knew there was something different about me, even before I had a name for it.

This "something different" expressed itself in a lack of interest in boys throughout high school and college. When I was asked out on a date, I usually politely refused. While I had lots of close male friends, there was a distinct lack of desire for anything more intimate than a good-bye hug after youth group. It was my friends who were female that captivated my heart and mind.

I couldn't make sense of this: Why didn't I feel the way my friends did? I was uninterested in dating, while my friends gushed about the dates they went on. While the walls of my friends' bedrooms were filled with pictures of David Cassidy or Bobby Sherman, mine were bare (except for pictures of the Carpenters—that should have been a clue). I didn't have any answers, so I threw myself into my school and church work. But something still nagged at me. What could it be?

Thinking back, I realize I had my hunches, but they were unarticulated and unformed. I can remember slyly making my way around library stacks and grabbing a psychology book from the shelf to read up on homosexuality. I didn't know why I was drawn to it, but I remember my breathing becoming quicker and shallow, and my cheeks reddening as I quickly skimmed the page. The book was slammed shut and quickly returned to the shelf if I heard footsteps, and as I passed a librarian or patron, I wondered if they could see something in me that I couldn't see in myself.

At the end of my first year of seminary, I literally ran away, hopping a Greyhound bus in Oakland and heading to Nova Scotia, where my grandparents lived. I lost myself in weeping, a tear-stained Bible on my lap, for the first 1,000 miles of that trip, until, finally emotionally spent, I claimed the part of me I most feared. I remember taking a deep breath and saying to myself, "I am a lesbian." Suddenly, God filled my life again and brought me peace.

My whole world suddenly made sense. All the angst I had experienced as a teen, all the pangs I felt toward certain friends, all my childhood crushes (even though I didn't realize that was what they were at the time) fell into place and I felt more complete, more whole, than ever before. I remember stepping down off the bus to the street where my mother was waiting for me, thinking, "I am a lesbian. I wonder if anyone can tell?"

I spent the summer painting my grandparents' home. It was a wonderfully meditative way to live into this new self-awareness. I wondered what impact it would have on my life and ministry.

I had always thought I would spend my ministry as a rural church pastor. I would live in a parsonage next to the church, be on the town's volunteer ambulance squad, and pray before significant high school events. Certainly, that is how my ministry began in Bloomville, New York, in 1983. Bloomville is a hamlet just north of the Catskill Mountains of New York. With a little more than 200 residents, it is a dairy farming community. The United Methodist Church there is the oldest Methodist Church west of the Hudson River to be in continuous use.

I was twenty-five when I arrived in Bloomville. I really did live next to the church. I drove the town ambulance. And I prayed before significant high school events. I loved the people of this small town and tried my best to serve them well. My ministry included lots of visitation, youth work, and growing the music ministry of the church. The parsonage stood in front of the church, standing out like a lighthouse beacon to passing motorists. It was fishbowl living at its finest.

In spite of this fishbowl, there was a part of me that was both public and hidden at the same time. I arrived at the parsonage with a partner.

I met Sandy while working on my clinical pastoral education (CPE) training at a California county hospital the summer before my final year of seminary. She was a physical therapist on the ward I served, and we immediately began a friendly, flirty banter. We became romantically involved and, after a year, we agreed to move to the East Coast together as I began my first appointment.

It was an incredibly bifurcated experience. This, however, was the norm for LGBTQ persons at the time. Our love was "the love that dare not speak its name."[12] The fullness of our lives was lived below the surface, unseen by most people. When in public, we were careful about our body language and personal space, lest the intimacy we shared give us away and make us vulnerable to attack. When traveling, only one of us would go into a hotel lobby to ask for a room, so that the clerk would not know that two women were seeking a room with one bed. There was fear of being denied a room or, even worse, being ridiculed, bullied, or assaulted.

Sandy was seen as my "friend." In fact, when I told the members of the church a friend would be living with me in the parsonage, they responded, "It's good to know you will have someone with you. The winters here are long and lonely." This small, country church understood the basic human need for companionship, and even though the full nature of our relationship was never disclosed, we were treated as a family. Whenever I was invited over for dinner at a parishioner's home, Sandy was invited. Together, we hosted an annual Christmas open house for the congregation.

While this semi-acceptance was welcomed, it was still hard living our life together largely in the closet. The burden this placed on our relationship took its toll, which ultimately resulted in the relationship ending shortly after I became a campus minister at San Francisco State University (SFSU).

I had become interested in campus ministry while pastoring in Bloomville. My district superintendent, the Rev. Bob Smyres, was a smart man: he saw the energy I had for ministry as someone in their mid-twenties and wanted to make sure I had opportunities to serve and grow beyond what my small church could offer. There was a campus ministry position available at the State University of New York at Delhi, just up the road from Bloomville, and he offered to adjust my appointment to half-time at Bloomville, half-time at Delhi. I jumped at the chance. A year into this arrangement, I heard more clearly a call to full-time campus ministry, so I began to work on a PhD at Drew University in Madison, New Jersey, to be better equipped to provide ministry in the academic setting.

My passion for evangelism grew out of my campus ministry experiences. While the common pattern had been for young people to drop out of church during their college years only to return once they started their own families, there was a whole generation that didn't return to church when they started having children in the mid-1960s. Now those children were in college. These young people had little to no church background. If we didn't find ways to reach them on their spiritual journey, another generation would be missing from the church.

In 1989, I moved to San Francisco to begin full-time campus ministry work. Campus ministry at San Francisco State University, a commuter school, was largely nine to five, Monday through Friday. When I wasn't guest preaching, I worshiped at Bethany United Methodist Church, in the Noe Valley section of San Francisco. Bethany was the fourth church to become a "reconciling congregation" (the term for churches in the UMC that are committed to the full inclusion of LGBTQ persons in the life and ministries of the church[13]). The church had a long history of engagement with the LGBTQ community and was half straight/ half LGBTQ. When the church was considering whether or not to declare itself a reconciling congregation, Foster

Stockwell, a straight lay leader in the congregation, said, "Look around. It's already who we are."

## OPEN IN MINISTRY

While I was serving as a campus minister in California, my clergy membership was still in the New York Annual Conference. Living in San Francisco and being three thousand miles away from home gave me some breathing room to live fully out of the closet. Living more openly was a requirement in a city like San Francisco, with such a vibrant LGBTQ community. The closet just didn't exist there. I couldn't have been as effective a campus minister if I had lived closeted.

This extended to my worshiping community at Bethany. As a parishioner, not a pastor, I was able to bring all of me to church without worrying about someone bringing a complaint against me for being a lesbian.

In the spring of 1992, a student came into my office and tossed me a copy of a lesbian magazine (think *People* magazine, but for and about lesbians). In the middle of the magazine was a half-page picture of me officiating at a holy union of two women. I broke out in a cold sweat—I may have been across the country from my home conference, but if this got back to the conference, I could be in great trouble.

A few weeks later, the San Francisco district superintendent, the Rev. Chuck Cordes, asked to see me. I broke out in a cold sweat again: Had he seen the picture, and was he going to send me back to New York? Then I thought, if he had seen the picture in a lesbian magazine, he would have more to answer to than I would!

When we finally met, I couldn't have been more surprised by the reason: he wanted to offer me a pastoral appointment.[14] "We have a church that has a unique community, and it's a challenge for us to find the right pastor. We think you're that pastor." The church was Bethany. It turned out that Bethany's pastor, the Rev. Kim Smith, was going to be appointed elsewhere. As the church began meeting with the district superintendent (DS) to discuss what it wanted in its next pastor, the members told the DS, "We'd like an openly lesbian pastor." To which the DS replied, "Well, we don't have any openly lesbian pastors in the UMC." The response by the congregation barely skipped a beat: "Then we want Karen Oliveto, but we know we can't have her because she is a member of the New York Annual Conference, not the California-Nevada Annual Conference."

When I met with Bethany's Staff Parish Relations Committee (SPRC) for my intake interview, they didn't know that I was the one they would be meeting. They practically fell off their chairs when I walked in the room and then proceeded to give me the toughest interview of my life! They were a congregation serious about their ministry and wanted to make sure I understood that.

As I took up my pastoral duties at Bethany, I did what I knew how to do as a parish pastor. I retreated into the closet. The SPRC called me into a meeting for what would be the conversation upon which my future rested. They said, "We asked the DS if you could be our pastor not in spite of being a lesbian, but because you are a lesbian, for that is where your pastoral strength comes from. And don't worry, we've got your back." I left that meeting committing myself to living as openly as possible. When Robin and I began dating seven years later, they welcomed her into the community with open arms.

Of course, this still required a dance between San Francisco's out-and-proud LGBTQ community and The United Methodist Church, which continued to tighten the squeeze on its LGBTQ members through increasing restrictions. It was clear what I could and could not say publicly. Sometimes, this created tension between me and some openly LGBTQ pastors and activists—who expected people to be out and proud. But I proved myself to be a vocal advocate for LGBTQ rights in church and society while working alongside these colleagues, and they respected my position with The United Methodist Church.

Bethany was a small, progressive church. Many members had attended seminary, and the community was committed to its spiritual growth and actively engaging in mission and justice work in the world. I originally anticipated serving there for a couple of years and then returning to New York. However, the relationship we developed, as pastor and parishioners, was so rich that I realized I was going to be there for quite some time, so I transferred my membership from the New York Conference to the California-Nevada Conference. I served at Bethany for twelve years and by the time I left, I had spent a quarter of my life there. In many ways, we grew up together, challenging each other to greater and greater faithfulness.

In February of 2004, I received a phone call from Michael Eaton, who excitedly informed me, "They are issuing marriage licenses to gay and lesbian couples at city hall!" A quick internet search confirmed this. Mayor Gavin Newsom had given approval to the city clerk to issue marriage licenses to all couples, regardless of sexual orientation. Michael asked if I would come to city hall and perform his marriage to Sean Higgins, his long-time partner. I had known the two of them for most of my ministry at Bethany, had worked and prayed with them, and had provided pastoral care as they sought to deepen their relationship. Of course I would marry them.

I headed down to city hall in a clerical collar and was unprepared for the scene before me: city hall had become a huge wedding chapel, filled with gay and lesbian couples getting married. Joy filled the rotunda, as every nook and cranny held a wedding party. As I stepped into city hall, several TV crews saw my collar and asked for an interview. At that moment, I became a public theologian, testifying to what I had seen and heard and how I understood this to be a holy experience of God.

I married Michael and Sean as well as nine other couples from the Bethany congregation. One couple, Dan and Wild Bill, desperately wanted to get married—no one knew how long the window of opportunity would remain open, since there were legal challenges to what was happening. They asked if they could be married on Saturday, but I was already committed to leading a daylong retreat. Then it hit me: the following day, Sunday, was Valentine's Day. We had already planned a recommitment of vows for all couples in the congregation. What if we included their wedding as part of the morning worship? Dan and Wild Bill were extravagant in their love for the members of the church. At Christmas time, they always found the biggest tree possible to adorn the sanctuary. They were always doing little things for the "LOLs." (Our senior women referred to themselves as the LOLs: "little old ladies" of the church. They were everyone's mother and grandmother.) When Dan was sick, the congregation rallied around both of them with prayers, love, and care. What better time or place for them to say their vows than before the community that loved them?

That Sunday, Dan and Wild Bill were joined in legal matrimony. We had decided to cancel Sunday school so that the children could be a part of the service. "Today, you are seeing something you will remember for the rest of your life," we told them, as this would be the first legal gay marriage ever conducted in a United Methodist Church building. TV stations captured the ceremony and showed excerpts during the evening news. It was one of the most powerful Sundays we had ever experienced.

The joy, for me, was short-lived. Within a few days, a complaint was filed against me from a member of the California-Nevada Annual Conference cabinet for performing Dan and Wild Bill's wedding. I had suspected a complaint would probably come from somewhere. But one can never really be prepared for the receipt of such a letter.

In the days that followed, I continued to provide a theological context for legal marriage for all loving couples. If 1 John is true, that God is love and love is of God, then God was positively busting out all over San Francisco during that "Winter of Love." I also thought long and hard about what might be the consequences for my actions. I could be reprimanded. I could lose my appointment. I could lose my ordination credentials. Did I do the right thing by marrying Dan and Wild Bill? Oh, yes.

My actions were based not on thumbing my nose at church rules, but because of my commitment to be a pastor to all in my care. To tell some that they were not worthy of my pastoral services would create second-class citizens in the household of faith. To tell gay and lesbian couples their love for one another and the life they shared was inferior to other members of my congregation would deny the mystery of God's love that flowed in and between them. Yes, I did the right thing, even if my denomination wasn't there yet.

The complaint process dragged on for many months, with no clear resolution in sight. I wasn't sure if I would be facing a church trial or not. In the middle of the waiting, Dr. Delwin Brown, acting dean of the Pacific School of Religion (PSR), asked to meet with me. He offered me the position of associate dean for academic affairs at the school. Not knowing the outcome of the complaint that still loomed over me, this felt like God's way of encouraging me in ministry, so I accepted the position. I started at the school in September of 2004. Later that month, the complaint against me was dropped.

Like I had experienced as a student, PSR had no closets. Here, too, I was able to live openly as I worked with faculty, staff, and students. I enjoyed this new ministry challenge, how it fostered my intellectual curiosity and enabled me to mentor students as they grew into their vocation. Retired bishop Bill Dew would frequently come into my office and we would chat about the state of United Methodism. As his health declined that year, Bill recommended that I teach the required classes for United Methodist ordination, and the following year I also taught the United Methodist history/doctrine/polity sequence as well as evangelism and mission.

The hardest part of this job was watching as some of my brightest and most passionate-about-ministry students were those who had left or were considering leaving The United Methodist Church. It didn't matter if they were straight or LGBTQ. Raised in an era when sexual orientation was simply a human variation, not an aberration, these students couldn't understand the church's stance. Rather than support what they saw as an unjust institution, they were seeking out more welcoming denominations, which by this time included nearly all other mainline Protestant denominations. LGBTQ students, who had never known a closet, were unwilling to live in one in order to serve through a church that had an unofficial policy of "don't ask, don't tell."

I loved the seminary setting, but after four years I was ready for more responsibility and challenge. I prayed to God, asking for vocational clarity. Then, out of the blue, I received a call from the Rev. Cecil Williams and Janice Mirikitani, from the iconic Glide Memorial United Methodist Church in San Francisco: "We'd like you to be our co-senior pastor." I politely said no and then had a quick conversation with God—"That's not the next step I'm looking for." Cecil, Jan, and board president Amy Errett were persistent. It took me nine months to say yes. I needed to be sure I had the gifts and skills Glide needed for this time in its life, when Williams, the leader who had made Glide what it is today, was aging. I needed to determine whether I had the spiritual stamina to pastor such a diverse congregation and the ego strength to be a co-senior pastor but not perceived as the leader, since Cecil was still in leadership, hired by the Glide Foundation and given the title minister of liberation after he reached mandatory retirement age within the UMC.

Once I was able to say yes to these three things, I told Cecil, Jan, and Amy that I was open to coming to Glide if the bishop, Beverly Shamana, felt it was in the best interests of the California-Nevada Conference, never dreaming that she would say yes. I was stunned when she agreed to the appointment, and on March 1, 2008, I became the co-senior pastor of Glide.

There were several challenges that I faced at Glide: I was a white person serving as a leader of an Afrocentric church; I was a woman in a church that solidly valued male leadership; and—ironically—I was not "out" enough for many of the LGBTQ members. Glide, while a United Methodist congregation, reflected San Francisco and truly lived into the words on its cornerstone: "A House of Prayer for All People." On any given Sunday, Glide is packed with more than two thousand people: church members, tourists, the curious, and the seekers. People with little to no religious background have had profound spiritual experiences here. Christians and non-Christians alike have found community and a spiritual home at Glide. Jewish persons make up about 15 percent of the congregation. Practicing Buddhists as well as atheists have given their testimonies in worship. Under Cecil's and Jan's leadership, Glide has grown into a congregation of 11,000 and a social service agency with eighty-seven programs.

So much of my leadership has been informed by my time at Glide. While I had studied liberation theology in seminary at Glide, it was put into practice, and the results were profound experiences of God's power and grace. The starting point for ministry at Glide is with those who reside on the margins. The goal is not to move the margins to the center in assimilation, but to move the center to the margins. The result is a hugely vibrant, transformative, and, yes, often chaotic experience of the Holy Spirit as those overlooked and/or oppressed by society find agency and voice. This lesson was foundational for me as I entered the episcopacy.

## GOD CONTINUES TO CALL

Over the years, parishioners and colleagues had urged me to consider the episcopacy. They felt I had the gifts needed for the work of bishop. I resisted considering it because I love the church and didn't want to harm it and I love my relationship with Robin and didn't want that to be harmed either. In 2016, however, my soul began to become restless. I felt that I had done what I could at Glide and was open to what God might want next. I had been sought out for interviews at a couple of places but had not been offered anything.

At the UMC General Conference in 2016, I realized that, as the senior pastor of one of the largest United Methodist churches in the United States, I had an important voice to bring to the conversations about the denomination's future. I wasn't sure what my participation might look like, so after General Conference, I began to pray about it in earnest.

People became more insistent that I consider the episcopacy. Two colleagues, the Rev. Kristin Stoneking and the Rev. Izzy Alvaran, gave me a deadline. Since the California-Nevada Annual Conference was less than a week away, they needed to know if I felt a call to the episcopacy so that they could help get the word out. Receiving an official endorsement from one's annual conference is an important step in the process. (While anyone can be nominated from the floor at jurisdictional conference, where the episcopal elections occur, having the endorsement of one's annual conference gets one's name on the initial ballot.) We agreed that we would talk on Sunday, June 12, and I would have a decision at that time.

Robin and I had a long conversation that Saturday night, weighing all the pieces: What gifts did I bring? Was this truly a call from God? Did we both feel called to it? Did I have a vision to bring to the ministry? We prayed about it and realized that much of our hesitancy came from a place of fear. In the middle of our discussion, Robin quoted

Scripture: "Perfect love casts out fear" (1 John 4:18b). That broke us both open, and we sat back in our chairs and just breathed slowly. Yes. Yes. Yes, there was a call. And yes, it was time to open ourselves up to it and see where it might lead.

We went to bed that night aware that later that next day, we would be informing our friends about a decision that had the potential to greatly change the direction of our lives. That morning, we woke up to the news of the Pulse nightclub shooting in Florida. In the early morning hours, a gunman opened fire in this gay nightclub, which was hosting "Latin Night." At the end of his rampage, forty-nine people were killed and fifty-eight wounded.

This act of violence against the LGBTQ community furthered my sense of call. The church's stance on LGBTQ lives invited physical, emotional, and spiritual violence. I had pastored in San Francisco a long time and had provided ministry to too many young people living on the streets who had been turned out of their homes by their "Christian" parents. I had cared for the spiritual wounds the church had inflicted on LGBTQ people. I had done the funerals of more than one person who could no longer live with the church's censure of their personhood and found relief by taking their own life. Instead of fear returning, the shooting deepened and broadened my sense of call: What difference could it make if an LGBTQ person was at the table at the Council of Bishops meeting? Homosexuality would no longer be an abstract "issue" to be debated.

I received the endorsement from my annual conference, and a couple of weeks later, the Western Jurisdiction Conference[15] was held in Scottsdale, Arizona. Nine of us were nominees for the position. Two of us—the Rev. Frank

Wulf and I—were LGBTQ. We nine did not see ourselves as "running" against each other. There was no sense of competition. Instead, we walked prayerfully together, as committed to discernment as the rest of the delegates were. From the very first ballot, I was the top vote-getter. However, being the top vote-getter isn't enough. To be elected, one has to receive a certain percentage of votes based on the number of votes cast. One by one, nominees began to drop out. Each nominee's withdrawal speech was spirit-filled and moved us all to tears. As the field of candidates grew smaller and it was evident that I was the clear front-runner, the lead delegates from each annual conference called for a closed session of just delegates—no visitors or media.

The delegates gathered together and were posed this question: "What would happen if we elected an openly LGBTQ person as bishop? How would this impact our churches, our conferences, our denomination?" By this time, I was the only LGBTQ candidate, so this was clearly a conversation about *me*. As people talked in small groups, the question was reformed: "What would happen if the most qualified candidate was LGBTQ and we *didn't* elect this person?"

There were just three candidates left: the Rev. Skip Strickland, the Rev. Dr. Dottie Escobedo-Frank, and me. The days had been long with constant interviews, and the Arizona heat was draining. I was extremely tired by that point. At one point, the three of us met with the inter-ethnic caucus. The Western Jurisdiction values the diversity present within our area. That meeting showed the difficult choice that exists when various marginalized groups are seeking representation in high levels of leadership. How do we hold that tension together? I remember watching Dottie respond to a question with great poise and grace. As I

listened to her wise words, I thought, "She will be a great
bishop." I felt tremendous peace. The gathering had been
an amazing experience of holy conferencing, and I was con-
tent knowing that Dottie would bring so much to the episcopacy. We returned to the plenary hall and Skip immediately
withdrew. That left Dottie and me. I was planning my own
withdrawal speech when Dottie began to move across the
room, a look of intense focus and peace on her face. She
stood before a microphone and spoke these words that are
etched forever in my heart and will guide my ministry:

> One scripture that has formed me is " . . . be cou-
> rageous, do not be afraid because I am with you." I
> ask my ethnic brothers and sisters who may feel like I
> deserted them to remember that I am always here and
> that we will not desert you! To my LGBTQ broth-
> ers and sisters that as in this moment you are being
> included in an extreme way, do not forget what it is
> like to be excluded . . . if we do not make a witness to
> the world, to be loving of the whole body of Christ,
> then why in the heck are we here? Brothers and sis-
> ters, if we are not united, we might as well pack it up.
> So this could divide us and the world would want us
> to think it will, but God is a God of miracles. This is
> a miracle if we can stay united. This is a miracle we
> cannot plan. It will take all of the love we have inside
> of ourselves to understand God created each and
> every one of us for this moment to love and show the
> rest of the world that we do not have to split because
> of theology.

On ballot 17, I was elected a bishop in The United
Methodist Church.

The rest is a blur as the delegates arose as one body, cheering and crying. We had walked a deeply spiritual path together. We had sat in silence, raised our voices in song, and prayed together, as we sought the guidance of the Holy Spirit. The joy in that room was palpable.

This was not the case in rooms across the country where other jurisdictions were holding their conferences. Because there was fear that indeed an openly LGBTQ person might be elected bishop, conservatives had crafted a generic question of law regarding the legitimacy of the nomination, election, consecration, and assignment of such a person. When my election was announced at the other conferences, delegates in two of the conferences brought forward for consideration this question of law. In the North Central Jurisdiction, it was tabled. In the South Central Jurisdiction, it was approved, but by a relatively slim margin. This meant that the "supreme court" of the denomination, the Judicial Council, would receive this question of law and provide a response.

This motion caused me to ponder so many questions: How could people who didn't know me, hadn't examined my qualifications, gifts, and skills, and had no firsthand experience of my ministry seek to disqualify me from this ministry? How could they reduce me to an issue for the Judicial Council to rule on? What does this say about our understanding of being a part of the body of Christ? Are any members expendable?

I have received cards, letters, and emails since my election that have filled several boxes. The overwhelming majority have been supportive. However, while some hearts experienced a healing from the election, others were broken by it. Their letters have been accusatory, "How dare you break apart the church?" and dismissive, "You are not a follower of Jesus Christ." Some have walked out of the room when I suggested we pray together. Instead of offering a charity of curiosity, they have judged me before knowing me.

This is symptomatic of a wide issue that pervades US culture. There is an "othering" of those who are different and an unwillingness to sit and share life together. We turn people into issues, which makes it easy for us to dismiss the experiences they seek to share with us, some of which might make us uncomfortable to hear. How is healing possible when we deny the humanness of the "other"? Where do we go from here?

Instead of an understanding that we are all one, worthy of mutual respect and equal rights, we fracture the human family with an understanding of who is in and who is out, who is like us, and who is different from us, who is us, and who is them. It is difficult if not impossible to define who we are without a corollary understanding of who we are not, which is how othering begins. Polish sociologist Zygmunt Bauman delineates othering in this way: "Abnormality is the other of the norm, deviation the other of law-abiding, illness the other of health, barbarity the other of civilization, animal the other of the human, woman the other of man, stranger the other of the native, enemy the other of friend, 'them' the other of 'us,' insanity the other of reason, foreigner the other of the state subject, lay public the other of the expert."[16] Once othering starts, however, it includes a hierarchy of value and a power differential. Certain attributes we share are of higher value than the other's attributes. Then, we get to not only define them, but determine what shall be made accessible and denied to them.

Currently, this othering is most evident in the public square conversation regarding the building of a wall and repeated attempts at a refugee ban. The darker the skin, the more to be feared. The more unlike our speech or religion, the more suspect. So we build a wall to keep us in and them out. We close borders, again to keep some in and others out. Even though the apostles Paul and Peter both learned that God keeps pushing borders wider, not to keep some out, but to include them, we fail to live this out in church and society. The essential divine oneness of creation and humanity is broken into a thousand sharp shards.

Does the truth of another's experience have to negate our own? Can there be multiple truths? Can we listen to lives that are different from ours and open ourselves to God's voice, which seeks to speak to us? The more we push away from each other, failing to recognize our common humanity, the more we allow misunderstanding, biases, and hatreds to flourish. All lives are diminished. When we stay at the table, even when differences may make us uncomfortable, we begin to truly feast on life's bounty God offers us. Just think of any church potluck you've been to: When everyone brings the same dish, even with their own unique twist to it, the potluck is a boring bust. But when everyone brings their favorite dish to the potluck, the table is filled to overflowing with flavors, textures, smells, and tastes. This is what God offers us in community with those who are unlike us. Our differences are holy and all our lives are sacred.

Chapter 2

# EXERCISING EMPATHY

The path from the Powell Street Station to the corner of Taylor and Ellis in the Tenderloin district of San Francisco, where Glide Memorial UMC stands, is a study in the disparity of wealth that exists in the United States. At Powell Street, tourists from around the world mingle with techies clutching the latest smart phone. Panhandlers wait with empty cups, asking for spare change. Most are ignored as pedestrians avert their eyes and walk quickly by.

Just a few blocks over, people stand in queues at Glide and St. Anthony's, waiting for a meal, or lie on the street, strung out on drugs. Some have created mini-camps, surrounded by all their possessions. Others just take their spot on an old piece of cardboard. Folks gather under street lamps, as money or the promise of sex is offered in exchange for drugs.

Most tour guides encourage sidestepping the Tenderloin, or the TL as it is known. As a pastor in the TL, I considered these forgotten and overlooked ones my congregation. As I walked through the neighborhood, people would greet me: "Hey, Rev!" "Hi, Momma Glide!" "See you Sunday, Pastor Karen!" I listened to the trials and hard times of my neighbors and celebrated their joys and milestones.

Thinking about those two worlds—Powell Street and the TL—I am struck by how I saw some of the best of humanity in what is considered one of the worst neighborhoods. Glide served food three times a day, 364 days a year (every day but New Year's Day), providing more than 800,000 meals. No matter what shape one was in—sick or stoned—or what one had done, there was a community ready to welcome you and food waiting for you. Even if it was past serving hours, bag lunches were kept at the front desk for anyone who asked for one.

One day, someone came to the front desk, asked for one of the bag lunches, and was informed that we had given out the last one. The person walked outside and began a loud, mournful wail. One person, sitting with his back against the wall of the church called out, "Hey, man! What's going on?" "I'm hungry. HUNGRY! And so tired. I need food" was the reply, given between sobs. The cries were from one who had reached the end of his rope, full of despair. "Hey now. C'mere. Look what I got." The man on the ground reached into his bag lunch and pulled out the sandwich. "It's not much, but I'll give you half."

The sobs quieted as the sandwich exchanged hands. The person slid down the wall and the two began to talk over their shared meal. I knew that if the scene had been closer to Powell Street, the hungry person would have stayed hungry. But one person felt the hunger pangs of another, and instead of turning away and hiding his own stash of food, he was moved to literally break bread with the hungry stranger.

Empathy is the ability to enter into the joys, pains, and experiences of another. Two people, sitting on a city sidewalk, one sharing a bag lunch with another, shows the power of empathy to fill hungry lives. Empathy creates community. It enables us to connect deeply with those who are different from us. Without empathy, differences and disagreements will surely lead to dismissiveness and division.

I believe that we are currently facing an empathy deficit in this country and, unfortunately, also in the church.

> Empathy is the capacity to understand or feel what another person is experiencing from within the other being's frame of reference, i.e., the capacity to place oneself in another's position. Empathy is seeing with the eyes of another, listening with the ears of another and feeling with the heart of another.[1]

However, while the global village is shrinking through social media and travel, there is a new provincialism emerging, resulting in the inability to understand another's experience and therefore give it validity. As a result, injustice increases and communication breaks down.

## EMPATHY BEYOND ONE'S RACE, CLASS, AND GENDER

One look at our city streets and how many cities have criminalized homelessness is an example of an empathy deficit. As someone who has worked with the homeless community, I learned that homelessness becomes a full-time job when you need to find a safe place to sleep, find food, find a place to go to the bathroom, brush your teeth, and attend to other personal hygiene matters. If we had empathy for those who were homeless, we would both seek to fix the systems that keep people in poverty and on the streets as well as find ways to make living on the streets more humane.

It is not unusual for Glide to have a fully packed church for its worship Celebrations, with people even sitting on windowsills and on the steps leading up to the chancel area. With so many people, particularly with many who are either high or mentally ill, there is always constant motion and a baseline noise level of people moving and muttering. I quickly became accustomed to this low hum of humanity around me as I preached. One day, I was preaching about the persistent widow who kept knocking on the judge's door seeking justice. I was mid-sermon and was only dimly aware that the hum was a bit louder and more agitated than usual. Cecil asked me to stop preaching for a moment. It was then that I realized there was a woman in the second pew in obvious distress. She was rocking back and forth and talking to herself. She began to get louder and louder and I could finally make out her words.

"F@#k this sh*t. F@#k this sh*t. F@#k this sh*t," she kept saying, over and over again. As I looked more closely at her, I realized she was one of the homeless folks Glide serves and invites into our community. "F@#k this sh*t."

I watched as Cecil made his way down to the second pew and sat himself down next to her. "F@#k this sh*t. No one knows how hard it is. No one! Not to be able to take a piss. Not to be able to clean myself up. Do any of the folks in this place know how hard it is when you are living in the streets?" She then began her mantra again: "F@#k this sh*t. F@#k this sh*t. F@#k this sh*t."

Cecil began to stroke her arm and then spoke to her, "We love you. We love you. We love you."

Back and forth, as two competing counterpoints, Cecil and the woman continued to speak: "F@#k this sh*t." "We love you." "F@#k this sh*t." "We love you." "F@#k this sh*t." "We love you." Slowly, Cecil's message of unconditional love began to reach her. Her words softened. She then began to cry as Cecil held her. After a few minutes, Cecil looked her in the eye for the longest time and said one more time, "We love you." The woman took a deep breath, exhaled, and sank into her pew peacefully. Cecil returned to his seat and motioned for me to continue my sermon.

The gospel came alive for us that morning as the woman in the second pew became the widow knocking at the door, persistent, relentless in seeking to be seen, heard, and responded to. We all *felt* her distress. We all *experienced* her struggle for dignity on the streets. We *suffered* with her. Her outburst wasn't an embarrassment. It wasn't something to be covered up or dealt with so that we could continue with the order of service. It was precisely why we gather: to know and be known by the God who loves us and the people who are our family, who bear witness to our struggles and tell us we are loved through it all.

But this is not the norm for most North American churches. The woman's expression of despair is not considered acceptable behavior in most public settings. People in physical, emotional, or spiritual distress are overlooked, unseen, and dismissed in society and politely escorted down the aisle and out the door of most churches. Our lack of empathy for another's lived reality breaks down human community. It limits our ability to engage one another in life-affirming ways that challenge and change unjust structures.

At Bethany United Methodist Church, where I served for twelve years, a similar scene had taken place, but with a much different outcome. Diana was a special needs child, adopted by Cheryl, a single mom. The church became the village that helped Cheryl raise Diana and two other children. We grew accustomed to Diana's questions that she'd ask during what many would consider inappropriate times. When she'd wander around the sanctuary, folks would watch her to make sure she was okay. Often, she would come up to the front of the sanctuary while I was preaching, and on more than one occasion I would pick her up and preach with her in my arms.

One Sunday, Diana was more agitated than normal. She spoke even more loudly and emphatically and would rarely stay seated. Finally, a visitor blurted, "Someone needs to do something about that child. She should be removed from the sanctuary."

You could have heard a pin drop after she spoke. I turned to the woman and said, "The only thing we will do with that child is continue to love her, so she will always know she is a child of God. We hope you will help us with that task." The woman got up from her seat and walked out the door. This was not our intent. Community can be messy, especially when people are invited to bring all of who they are to it.

Another example of a lack of empathy is shown when white, presumably heterosexual men decide they know what is best for women's health care and reproductive rights. Pictures of Republican politicians creating laws that will impact women's lives, with no women at the table, show what can happen when we fail to have empathy—we create policy that affects the lives of others with no input or guidance from the very people whose lives will be impacted.

In late 2017, the #MeToo movement emerged in the United States. Beginning with those in the entertainment industry, women began to name not only the sexual harassment and assault they had experienced, but also the names of their abusers. More and more women began to share their stories, as social media was filled with #MeToo testimonies. From politicians to movie directors, men began to be held accountable for their abusive actions toward women. Some of the abusers were penitent. Others couldn't understand what the fuss was about. Still others wondered, "If these acts really happened, why did it take these women so long to say something?"

A lack of empathy enables one to treat another as an object, meant for one's own pleasure or power. Sexual harassment/abuse fails to understand the impact one's behavior has on the one being abused. It has no concept of how the behavior shames and harms. It can take years for an abused one to finally name the behavior. Someone who asks why it took so long for the abuse to be named fails to have empathy for the one who was harmed, to note the visible and invisible scars that create a deafening silence.

Perhaps more than any issue, race relations in the United States provides evidence of the empathy deficit we face. Whites have difficulty seeing beyond the privilege their race affords to seeing those whose experience is much different. Racial discrimination is often discounted or denied. There is an inability or lack of will to open oneself up to the real lived experience of another.

This was one of my deepest lessons as pastor of Glide. As a white woman, I had to confront my privilege, and the fact that my walk in the world is much easier because of my race than the walk of persons of color. Every day, I had to confess my racism. Racism is so deeply embedded in our culture and entangles all of us in its web of inequity. Racism isn't an inconvenient social construct. It is a deadly way to control others.

Too many of us who live comfortably and even blindly with the privilege that comes from our white skin want to stick our heads in the sand and pretend that we live in a post-racial society. When we hear our black and brown brothers and sisters tell of their racist treatment, we often interrupt and say, "It's not really like that anymore." Or, "You should see what happened to me."

I have to consciously reject my racism every day, and the main way I do so is through the power of empathy, listening deeply to how those of color have a much different experience of the world than I do. I must understand that doors that open up automatically for me because of my whiteness open with difficulty—if at all—for persons of color. My race affords me places of safety not granted to those of other races. I am not frightened of police officers. I don't worry that by putting on a hoodie, I will be perceived as dangerous. I have never given my nieces and nephews "the talk" about how they should behave if ever stopped by a police officer. I have never been followed in a store by the owner because he automatically assumes that I am a suspect for shoplifting simply because of the color of my skin. I have never had to look very far—in books, movies, television, or church meetings—to see people who look like me. In white America, the color of my skin grants me power and privilege.

I will never forget the day I realized that my walk in the world was different from that of my friends of color. In college, one of my professors (yes, one) was black. Every day he came to class dressed so dapper. In an era when jeans and flannel shirts were the rule, he stood out by his three-piece suits and hat, even though he was only about five years older than the students he taught. There was a reason why he dressed so fine. It was a way to show respectability in a culture that held black men with suspicion. He told us about how not once, not twice, but nearly every time he drove through the town to get to work, he would be pulled over by police. This wasn't Birmingham in the 1950s—it was New Jersey in the 1970s. Whether he was with a colleague or his children, he would suffer the indignity of the police asking him to step out of the car for questioning. His crime? Guilty of driving while black.

This busted open my world. I didn't question the truth of his experience. I didn't try to dismiss it. Instead, it forced me to see my own privilege and began my commitment to be an ally in dismantling racism. From Birmingham of the 1950s to New Jersey in the 1970s to San Francisco in the 2010s, there is still much work to do.

One day, I was nearly to the door of Glide when a taxi pulled out and Joyce Hayes fell into my arms sobbing. Joyce was the matriarch of the church. I asked what was wrong, and she said she had been standing at the curb at the Ferry Building for forty-five minutes, trying to hail a cab. Literally hundreds of taxis passed her by without stopping. Finally, a white man noticed what was going on and asked if he could help. He raised his hand and immediately a cab stopped. The stranger had empathy for an elderly black woman who was simply trying to hail a cab. That empathy propelled him to take action, to stand with the woman and use his own privilege to assist her.

Empathy between oppressed groups is often in short supply, as we each strive for our own group's rights and opportunities. I saw this tendency in action when our friends Gail and Donna came to visit us in San Francisco. Gail, an African American, wanted to get a T-shirt from an LGBTQ organization. When we went into the store, Gail went straight to the back of the store, where the T-shirts were. The rest of us—all white—stayed in front. Immediately, one of the cashiers went to the back. I assumed he was going to help my friend find the sort of shirt she was looking for, so I went back to help her look as well. Instead of helping Gail, however, he had profiled her and was trying to inconspicuously follow her, to make sure she wasn't going to steal something.

When we left the store, she was livid at her treatment. Being a community leader in San Francisco and in the LGBTQ community, I wrote to the organization's executive director, explaining what my friend experienced and I witnessed, and suggesting that the organization bring in someone to train their workers on cross-cultural competency and intersectionality. Instead of an apology, the executive director replied, "There's no way this could have happened in our store!"

As the Rev. Dr. Dottie Escobedo-Frank implored when the Western Jurisdiction elected me, a lesbian, instead of her, a Latina, we must not forget what it feels like to be excluded, but rather let our experience with exclusion grow our empathy for others on the margins. When we refuse to hear the truth of the lived experiences of others, we become oppressors, exercising power over others. We see it as a way to keep ourselves "safe." At least that's what we convince ourselves we are doing.

It was early in my ministry at Glide that I had an epiphany of my own lack of empathy, which was limiting my understanding of those whose lives were so different from my own. As we studied the demographics of Glide's neighborhood, we discovered that the largest concentration of the formerly incarcerated in San Francisco was located within a two-block radius of Glide. We discussed what we should do in response. Then we realized we were asking the wrong question. We began to ask, What can those who are formerly incarcerated teach us of their lives and tell us how we can be in partnership with them to assist them in their transition to life "on the outside"?

We passed out flyers around the neighborhood, inviting folks to come to a free dinner and open mic night. Glide's Freedom Hall was packed with people. One by one, guests moved to the microphone and shared the reality of their lives. In the telling alone, empowerment was found. It was such a powerful night, we decided to host a "Speak Out" every week.

Each Wednesday, an amazing collection of humanity gathered: homeless and housed, addicts and those in recovery, sex workers and Glide staff, congregants and tourists came together to tell the truth of their lives. One evening, a young man wove his way to the microphone and swayed in silence in front of us. His rotting teeth exposed the depth of his addiction. His glassy eyes and twitching body gave away the fact that he was quite high. The usual noise around the room settled the longer he stood in silence at the microphone. When the room was totally quiet and all eyes were on him, he looked at us and said, "Can I trust you with my dignity?"

Those words have been seared into my soul. This really is the heart of it all. Can others trust me with their dignity? Can I see beyond my own reality and truth and embrace the fact that the reality and truth of others doesn't discount my own? It does, however, inform my life and invites me to live in ways that are responsive to the pains and sufferings of others.

This insight has been helpful as I navigate difficult conversations with those angry at my election. My task is not to defend or debate. My task is to listen. How has my ministry adversely impacted the faith of others? How can I respond in ways that build relationship, not further alienate and separate? What is it about my election that has aroused such anger?

### STAYING UNDEFENDED AND GENEROUSLY LOVING

As I engage with those unhappy with my election, I am always surprised at not just the hurtful ways they feel they can address me, but their unwillingness to acknowledge my personal faith journey. I discussed this with my spiritual director, the Rev. Debra Peevey. Debra was the first and only out LGBTQ pastor in her denomination for nearly a decade. She shared with me a conversation she had with a pastor who had had a conversion experience from condemning LGBTQ persons to becoming an ally. She asked him, "What did you think of us as you were saying those hateful things about us and our lives? Did you ever think of how you were harming us?" He responded, "To tell you the truth, I never once considered your humanity."

I have experienced this in my role as bishop. As part of my commitment to be in ministry with all people, as well as to get to know my episcopal area, I asked my district superintendents to take me on a tour of our area's churches so I could meet people and learn of their ministries. I never knew how I would be received by these communities. Would people welcome me as their bishop, or would they be hostile? As we pulled into the parking lot of each church, I prayed this prayer: "Keep me undefended, O God, and help me be generously loving in all I say and do." Almost always, I was received warmly by the churches. As I stepped in one church, however, I realized I was facing a hostile crowd.

As I entered the room, sixty people were in neat rows facing away from the door. Everyone had a Bible, pad of paper, and pen on their lap. No one smiled. No one acknowledged me. The pastor introduced the Rev. Margaret Gillikin, the district superintendent, and me. Margaret gave the usual introduction, which included a little about my background and the purpose of our visit. Then I stood before the crowd to speak. There were two questions I asked every church: "How are you making disciples of

Jesus Christ for the transformation of the world?"—which is based on the mission statement of The United Methodist Church—and "How can I as your bishop and the staff of the annual conference serve you better to support you in your ministries?" Between the two questions, I usually offered a small devotion.

I had barely stated the first question when people began interrupting me in angry tones, questioning me regarding my understanding of the Bible and the church. Every time I tried to respond, someone would cut me off, dismiss my answer, and ask another question. It was an aggressive, hostile interrogation, and my responses were clearly unacceptable.

I realized that we were not going to engage together in healthy dialogue, so I said, "It's time for Margaret and me to head to the next church. Let's pray together first." As I bowed my head, I heard chairs being shoved aside as voices clamored, "We will *not* pray with you." "No *way*." "You can pray on your own." When I finished my prayer, a room that once held sixty people now held ten.

How would this encounter have been different if empathy had guided our interaction with one another? Empathy causes our defenses to come down and our guardedness to yield to generosity and honest curiosity. It encourages an inquiry that invites further discussion and discovery through mutually respectful engagement. Instead, brokenness was furthered by an unwillingness to remain at the table together and be in prayer with and for one another.

Another experience where a lack of empathy was exposed was at a meeting of the Council of Bishops. During this twice-yearly meeting, United Methodist bishops from around the world gather to attend to the spiritual needs and administrative oversight of the church. I was extremely nervous about attending my first council meeting, knowing that there were some bishops unhappy with my election. I was greatly relieved by the warm welcome of my new colleagues and enjoyed being a part of the council.

The second meeting of the council occurred following the April 2017 meeting of the denomination's Judicial Council, where the question of law regarding my election was considered. The council would rule on the question by the end of the week, when we bishops were gathering for our meeting in Dallas. The Judicial Council's ruling could abruptly change the course of my life: Would I still be a bishop? Would I still be assigned to the Mountain Sky Area? Would I still have an income and place to live? Robin and I lived into this uncertainty in the months prior to the decision by sinking into God's embrace and trusting that God had brought us this far and wouldn't abandon us.

When the Judicial Council ruled on the eve of the start of the Council of Bishops meeting, I was relieved that my consecration and assignment were still in place. However, their decision added new restrictions to LGBTQ people in ministry, and I was concerned about how this would impact my relationship with bishop colleagues.

At this meeting, all new bishops were going to be formally presented to the council, since both newly elected US and non-US bishops were now in place. Each new bishop would be receiving an official parchment, personalized with our deacon and elder ordination dates and the date of our episcopal consecration, along with the names of the bishops who participated in each event. At the beginning of our meeting, all the new bishops' parchments were laid out, so that all bishops could sign them. All bishops queued up and began to move from parchment to parchment in order to sign them, one after the other.

In the middle of our council meeting, members of the executive team called me aside. "We have noted what happened with your parchment and want to order a new one." I had anticipated that some bishops would refrain from signing my parchment and attempted to shrug it off: "That's okay. You don't have to do that." They responded, "We are troubled by how people defaced your parchment, and we want to correct this."

Wait . . . defaced?

Sure enough: there, on the signatures section of the parchment, two bishops had realized they had accidentally signed my parchment as they were moving through the line and had gone back to cross their names out. One name was still plainly visible. The second name was painstakingly crossed out to ensure that it was illegible. Thirteen other bishops had not signed my parchment.

It is those two bishops who crossed out their names that I have reflected on the most. Did these two individuals stop and consider how their actions would affect me? Did they pause before scratching their names out, wondering how their etching would look on this official parchment, one that would hang in my office and eventually be sent to The United Methodist Archives? Did they ever stop to consider my feelings as they sought to erase the tacit approval their signature gave of my episcopacy? Where was their empathy toward a colleague they might have held reservations about but was nonetheless still a colleague? Debra's conversation with her colleague helps me understand their actions: "I never once considered your humanity."

But I, too, have to ask myself, "Where and when do I deny another's humanity?" I know my election has caused some to question their faith, their reading of Scripture, their understanding of rules as well as the church. There are times when I get weary and impatient of those who struggle with my election. When I feel these emotions rising up within me, I take it as a nudge from God, a reminder to exercise empathy, to feel their sense of loss and confusion, and to make that the starting point in my relationship with them.

The heart of the gospel of Jesus Christ reduces all the laws to two: to love God and love others. But without an integration of empathy and love, we continue to "other." It is what fosters the saying "Hate the sin but love the sinner," or, the ultimate in passive-aggressive love, "Bless your heart."

We need a spirituality that increases our capacity for empathy. We need to foster this in every faith community, in our schools, in our workplaces, in our families. We need to learn spiritual practices and spiritual disciplines that open us to the depth of empathy that connects us to the experiences faced by others in the human family.

Empathy isn't an easy thing to master. Like any muscle, it requires practice and constant exercising. Without doing so, empathy atrophies. We measure the rest of the world, including the experiences of others, against our own life experiences. We can grow our capacity for empathy by being curious about others and allowing their lives to speak instead of viewing them through the lens of our own life.


### WELCOMING A SISTER

At Bethany, I saw a community move from questionable toleration to embracing another's humanity through empathy's and love's integration. Bethany was proud of its long history in the gay/lesbian movement for equality and justice. Gay and lesbian members were community leaders in San Francisco as well as in the denomination. The members considered themselves progressive and inclusive . . . until the first openly transgender person became a part of the community. Molly tested the limits of Bethany's openness and caused the congregation to struggle with a new layer of issues around inclusivity.

There are three distinct moments that stand out for me, when there was a concrete expression of empathy that helped the congregation embrace Molly and all of who she was. The first was an event of a newly formed women's group. It was held at the backyard pool of one of our members. The announcement was made in church, inviting all the women of the congregation to this special event. Molly signed up. At this point, Molly had only just begun hormone treatment. She was still living her life as a man professionally. In fact, church was the only place she was exclusively living as a woman. While her hair was long and she used quite a bit of makeup, physically, she was still very much a male. Her desire to attend the women's group gathering raised questions for some of the women: Did we really accept Molly as another woman in the church? What made one a woman?

Even though some women struggled with these questions, all encouraged Molly to attend the event. We all knew that this would be Molly's first outing in a woman's bathing suit. She arrived a little late. We were already soaking in the tub. We tried to maintain our conversation as Molly disrobed to reveal a woman's one-piece suit. Then, as she plunged into the hot tub, our admiration of her courage moved us beyond questions of who is a woman and who is not. We cheered as she broke the surface. We were able to experience her vulnerability as well as her courage, and it connected us with her deeply. We knew this hot tub immersion was truly a baptism of water and the Spirit, as Molly claimed yet again who God had created her to be.

The second time was the first church retreat Molly attended with us. We were in a lodge that had two dormitories filled with bunk beds. As people were choosing their beds, it became evident that we had created one male bunkroom and one female bunkroom. Those of us who arrived early wondered where we should "put" Molly. Then we realized our arrogance—we were not "putting" anyone anywhere—retreatants were choosing for themselves their sleeping quarters. Molly should be allowed to do the same. This was the greatest lesson Molly taught us: the importance of allowing someone to name themselves. Even as an "open" congregation, we had to confess our own rigid adherence to societal norms of what made a person male or female. We struggled with our desire to have people fit into certain categories, while Molly's presence reminded us of the mystery of sexuality and gender. Molly helped us to hold in reverence this sacred gift and to meet people where they were in their journey of claiming their own piece of this gift.

Every Sunday, Molly sat near the church's Little Old Ladies—the LOLs, as they called themselves. Molly had chosen her place in worship nearest the group that had the hardest time understanding who she was. These women, most of them over eighty, grew up in an era when there was no ambiguity about gender or sexuality. Gender roles and expectations were clear and rigid. Yet, in their midst, Molly found a worship home. One Sunday, during the sharing of joys and concerns, Molly announced that she had had her license officially changed from male to female. Instantly, her pew mates broke into applause. These LOLs embraced her and accepted her, even when they couldn't fully understand her.

Perhaps this is the deepest gift of empathy: it doesn't require us to figure out or understand someone else's life or experiences. Figuring out and understanding always happens through the lens of our own experience. A person's life is translated through what we know. Empathy, instead, allows us to *feel* what another is experiencing. It doesn't reduce or diminish another's experiences because of what we know or don't know. It accepts that person in her totality and enables us to then love unconditionally. This is one of the lessons Molly taught me as her pastor.

None of the other churches I had served had ever had a transgender member, at least that I was aware of. Molly, wanting me to understand her life and struggles, gave me lots of reading material, primarily autobiographies by other transgender people. While there were common threads in each story, nothing helped me understand better than Molly herself.

Pastoral relationships, no matter who they're with, require us to be open to the life experiences of another and to discern there the movement of God. Empathy is necessary if we are to do it well. Molly's life experiences were vastly different from my own, but I was committed to meeting her where she was and being her companion in the faith. This was not always easy. There were parts of her world that were tremendously unfamiliar to me. There were communities she belonged to that were far from my own. So that our relationship could have integrity, I did not hide either my ignorance or my lack of understanding from Molly.

Molly returned my honesty by being patient with me as she took great pains to educate me. More than anything,

Molly wanted to be known, especially by the faith community. The most difficult area for me, however, was around gender issues. Molly, as she explored what it meant for her to be a woman, pressed a lot of my buttons around my own feelings of inadequacy and around my questions about gender. While Molly was asking her own set of questions, a voice within me was asking, "So, what does it mean for you, Karen, to be a woman?" It would have been easy to take out my own frustrations on Molly. I knew I had my own work to do around these issues so that I could be as present as possible to Molly and not have my own issues set the agenda for our time together. This was especially important in light of what I represented to Molly. She had known much rejection from the church and had been taught to be ashamed of who she was. Yet she knew that God, for whatever reason, had made her who she was. By representing the institutional church, I could be a vessel of healing for Molly, as she struggled between the church's rejection and God's acceptance.

In order to know her beyond my own frame of reference, Molly forced me to scale what sociologist Arlie R. Hochschild refers to as an "empathy wall," which she describes as

> an obstacle to deep understanding of another person, one that can make us feel indifferent or even hostile to those who hold different beliefs or whose childhood is rooted in different circumstances. In a period of political tumult, we grasp for quick certainties. We shoehorn new information into ways we already think. We settle for knowing our opposite numbers from the outside. But is it possible, without changing our beliefs, to know others from the inside, to see

reality through their eyes, to understand the links between life, feeling, and politics; that is, to cross the empathy wall?[2]

In her book *Strangers in Their Own Land: Anger and Mourning on the American Right*, Hochschild set out to scale her own empathy wall. In many camps, Hochschild would be considered a political and intellectual elite: as a child, she grew up amidst cultural diversity as the daughter of a US ambassador who was assigned to New Zealand, Tunisia, and Ghana. Her higher education includes degrees from prestigious schools on both the East and West Coasts. Since 1971, she has been a professor of sociology at the University of California, Berkeley.

She spent five years studying the American Right, trying to understand the political fault line that has revealed itself in American politics in the twenty-first century. To do that, she had to catch her own biases and assumptions and listen openheartedly to those whose worldviews were so different from her own.

She chose Louisiana to be her laboratory, mainly because demographics showed it to be as far from her personal experience as she could get: Southern, white, evangelical, anti-Obama. She hoped to climb over her own empathy wall by turning "my own political alarm system off and actually try and see how it felt to be them."[3]

In the five years of her study, Hochschild interviewed sixty people, forty of whom were Tea Party members. As she got to know the people in the study, she quickly became aware of the wall between them. Most often, we simply accept the wall and place whatever new knowledge we discover about others within the framework of our own experience. Hochschild wanted to create a bridge over the wall.

By exploring the deep stories told by another—the feelings that reside in the story, where fears, shame, resentment, hopes, pride, and anxiety are revealed. It is through this emotional connection that one can receive the fullness of another's story without having to give up one's own positions.

There are more walls being created these days than bridges. We have lost the capacity to listen to one another, to be open to the truth another brings to the conversation. We stand ready to rebut, rebuke, and reject. Theologian Nelle Morton said that we are to "hear one another into speech."[4] This deep listening allows the deep stories to emerge. Words can flow without censure, because they are being received by one not ready to discount them, but instead open to the meanings and feelings behind the words.

Mutual transformation occurs when we listen to one another at a heart level, with a willingness to be surprised, challenged, and moved by another's experience. The bridge is created, the wall is overcome, and empathy is reclaimed as relationships are restored.

### THE POWER OF WORDS

Pastoral relationships require me to climb the wall and build the bridge, over and over again. One of the members of a church I served came from Oklahoma. He loved The United Methodist Church. When he came out as a gay man, he was blessed to find a church in that area that was a reconciling congregation—one that had made a public commitment to be in ministry with and for all people, regardless of sexual orientation or gender identity. When Jeff's work reassigned him to San Francisco, finding another reconciling congregation to join was one of the first things he did.

Jeff became not only an active member but also a leader in the congregation. His faith was strong, his spirituality deep. He loved The United Methodist Church and the way it fostered his relationship with God. Even though the denomination had pronounced that his sexuality was "incompatible with Christian teaching," the Wesleyan means of grace, by which we come to draw closer to God and follow Jesus more faithfully, were stronger than these words of condemnation.

Years passed, and I was no longer serving that congregation when I received a call from Jeff. It was 2012, shortly after The United Methodist Church's General Conference, held every four years. Jeff had listened intently to the debates at General Conference regarding homosexuality. For him, and other LGBTQ persons, the debate wasn't around an issue; it was about us—our lives, our loves, our faith, and our place in the household of God. He yearned, as we all did, to hear the church finally recognize us as beloved children of God, siblings in Christ.

Some of the delegates were a welcome balm. Jen Ihlo, a lay delegate from the Baltimore/Washington Conference, reminded the church: "I want to be clear that this is not an abstract issue. This is about people who are being harmed by the church and by the use of the 'incompatibility' language. I am a lesbian and a child of God and I strongly urge the body to support this compromise language so that gay youth . . . will recognize that the church loves them and God loves them and the violence and pain and suicide will stop."[5]

Unfortunately, he also heard other voices seeking to reaffirm the negative language. More than that, he heard one delegate from Africa rise to state that he "refused to accept" the assertion that LGBTQ individuals were made that way by God. "Because God is a loving God, he cannot create a person with something that would make him or her suffer," he said. At one point during the man's speech, the translator—translating from Swahili—was so upset by the man's words that he actually apologized to the delegates for what the man was saying, for the delegate compared homosexuality to bestiality.[6]

Words like this harm. Words like this create a wall instead of a bridge. They deny the truth found in another's life and instead perpetuate falsehoods that damage not just individuals but communities.

For Jeff, a middle-aged white Christian man, it created a wound too deep for repair. He called me with one question, "Pastor, how can I be unbaptized?" His question crushed me. Baptism, for me, is an important sacrament that shows God's deep and abiding love for us. Just as Jesus, when rising from the Jordan River after John baptized him, heard this affirmation from on high, "This is my Son, the Beloved, with whom I am well pleased" (Matt. 3:17), we, too, are God's beloved children. We, too, receive this affirmation at our baptism.

This baptism marked the start of a new chapter in Jesus' life. The Gospels retell the stories of Jesus' ministry following his baptism. However, at the time of his baptism, what miracle had Jesus performed at that point in his life? Who had he healed? Who on the margins did he defend? Jesus had done none of it. Nothing. He was a carpenter, like his father, Joseph. What had he done to warrant this pronouncement, this love, this pride, this affirmation from on high? "This is my Son, the Beloved, with whom I am well pleased." Nothing out of the ordinary, nothing that was worth placing in the Gospel story for us to read about. The extraordinary work Jesus did in the world followed his baptism. Jesus was loved for simply being Jesus.

I love baptism. I especially love baptizing babies, because when we baptize a baby we are reminded of something of the nature of God. There is nothing a baby has to do to earn love. She doesn't have to be a good girl; he doesn't have to behave in any particular way. Just by being, a baby is loved. This is what baptism is about: you are loved, and there is nothing you can do about it.

When Jeff asked to be unbaptized, it broke my heart and I felt within me an anger I had never felt before. The church failed him. It failed him because it negated the truth that he is deeply loved by God who offers each of us the same affirmation that was offered to Jesus: we are loved not because of what we do, but because of who we are. The church broke its promise to him, made at the time of his baptism, to love him no matter what. At the time of our baptism, the community makes a promise to God and to us as well, that it will commit to remind us what we might forget: that we are unconditionally loved and unconditionally accepted. It doesn't matter if you turn out gay or straight, an addict or an accountant, or an addicted accountant. Our task, as brothers and sisters, is to provide a reminder of this love whenever one of us forgets.

The current debate over homosexuality requires us to "get over the wall" and build a bridge through empathy. The soul violence that The United Methodist Church is inflicting on its LGBTQ members is a sign of our inability to understand that words have power. Whoever said "Sticks and stones may break my bones, but words can never hurt me" is living in a state of deep denial. Words do hurt. Words do harm. Our words have the ability to bolster up another, or to pull the rug out from their feelings of self-worth. A report by the University of Maryland[7] found that 97 percent of young people hear anti-LGBTQ remarks in their schools. LGBTQ youth in the study report that 84 percent have been verbally harassed. As a result of the harmful messages they receive, LGBTQ youth are at a greater risk for substance abuse, homelessness, and self-harm. LGBTQ youth are four times more likely to attempt suicide than their straight peers (33 percent, compared to 4 percent).

Words harm.

Empathy enables us to understand the power behind our words. By climbing the wall and building a bridge, we can have a greater understanding of how our words impact another's life, because we have allowed ourselves to see the world through their eyes—their pains, hopes, fears, and hurts inform our own behavior. We have done what Atticus Finch in *To Kill a Mockingbird* advises his daughter, Scout, to do: "First of all," he says, "if you can learn a simple trick, Scout, you'll get along a lot better with all kinds of folks. You never really understand a person until you consider things from his point of view […] until you climb into his skin and walk around in it."[8]

I wrote much of this book while in Nova Scotia, where I have spent nearly every summer of my life, close to family and friends. One evening, we were gathered with my Uncle Howie, Mary Dee MacPherson, and her adult children, Tony and Kim. Someone asked me about this book. I spoke of how I believe we are experiencing an empathy deficit and the result is a crisis of community. My listeners looked at me quizzically, as if I was speaking a foreign language. Then, Mary Dee said, "Oh! You're talking about the States! Not Canada." We continued the conversation as we

sought to understand why the lack of empathy seems to ⌐.
at epidemic levels in the United States and yet not so much
in Canada. What we recognized was that the starting point
in Canada is the community: how can we each do our part
to keep the common body as healthy as possible? Whereas
in the United States, the starting point is the individual: "I"
not "us" guides personal and communal decision making.

Community requires empathy if it is to be a healthy
community. Without empathy, community is held together
by impersonal systems and organizations rather than
relationships of mutuality and trust. A community held
together by rules instead of relationships results in majority
thinking: "My way is the best way, and since so many others feel like I do, this is the right way." The problem with
majority thinking is that the minority—whose experiences,
needs, and concerns are overlooked and/or dismissed—are
usually the most vulnerable.

Empathy helps us get beyond majority thinking. It
helps us see that "my way" isn't the only way. When that
happens, we begin to live into the tension that diverse realities creates. This tension is not to be avoided but embraced,
for it is in living through the tension that we are brought to a
deeper place of community.

# Chapter 3
# LEANING INTO AMBIGUITY

When we gain empathy, we enter into the pains and joys of another. We begin to see the world with new eyes, beyond our own reality. Empathy pushes our understandings of right and wrong action and calls into question our own experiences and understandings of the world. Perhaps this is what makes diversity without division such a difficult exercise. There seems to be within human nature a desire for certainty. Our educational systems foster this notion. The quality and quantity of our knowledge is rated on what we know to be true and what we know to be false.

Much of life, in Western culture, is broken down into binaries, two categories that are in opposition to each other: yes/no; up/down; right/left; here/there. In binary thinking, there is a hierarchy of value, with one category given power or dominance over the other. With binary thinking, those with power get to denote preferences that have far-reaching implications. For instance, "*male* is better than *female*," "*white* is better than *black*," "*Western culture* is better than *non-Western culture*," "*heterosexuality* is better than *homosexuality*."

The problem with binary thinking is that it is not an accurate reflection of reality. The world is not made up of two opposing alternatives. These categories fail to take in the complexities of the world. Binary thinking reduces our capacity to hold difference in tension and limits our thinking and thereby the choices we make in life. There is little to no room for the gray area.

However, much of life is lived in the gray area. It seems as if as we grow older, the gray area becomes larger. For some, this gray area is uncomfortable because it forces a deeper engagement from us. It challenges assumptions and ways of being and doing. When confronted with the gray areas, we shut ourselves down or long to return to a far simpler time, back to the clarity of binary thinking.

Most of the time, the gray areas are uncomfortable, because they cause us to inhabit a space where the right or wrong action or truth/untruth aren't so obvious and our own understandings of reality are brought into question and challenged.

My parents split up when I was a young child. I couldn't comprehend why this happened. Truly, I never remember my parents ever fighting with one another. I do remember both parents at separate times sitting me down and explaining that my father would no longer be living with us but we'd still see him often. As a child, this news didn't make sense to me: If they weren't fighting, why would they not want to live together?

We did see my dad most nights. He would arrive sometime after dinner, and he would spend time with us until we went to bed. Sometimes, my dad would create timed math challenges for us, which we would do over and over, trying to beat our own times. Other times, we would play games. We would go to the library, amusement parks, and the beach. We'd fish, play chess, and visit Grandma Oliveto in Astoria, Queens. Daddy was still very much in our lives, even if he no longer resided with us.

I remember when Alisa, one of my best friends who lived on the same block, asked me why my father didn't stay the night. I can remember the exact spot where she asked that question—right at the corner of our street, Blanchard Street, and Great East Neck Road, in front of the Reynolds' house. When she asked it, I can still recall all the air leaving my lungs. I honestly didn't know. All I knew was what my parents had told me, "Daddy won't be living here anymore." I remember my cheeks burning as my mind raced for an answer: "Oh, he works late so he stays at a hotel so he won't come home and wake us in the middle of the night." Instead of uttering those words that are so terrifying for so many—"I don't know"—I made up something I could believe to be true.

This is my first memory of having something not "fit" in my worldview, so I made something up to make it fit, to escape the anxiety of not knowing. Instead of asking my parents to explain the situation a little better, I decided to make up my own reality about the situation. The desire for certainty about my own belief of the situation was stronger than my desire to know what was really going on.

It is not only children who do this. We as adults do this all the time. Sometimes this uncertainty comes from lack of information, as it did for me that day on the street corner, but many times, uncertainty emerges when we are presented with information or experiences that challenge our current way of thinking. We tend to assume that the way we experience the world is how everyone else experiences it, and that what is obvious to us is obvious to everyone. In this black-and-white paradigm, those who view the world differently are discounted or dismissed. We can't both be right, we think, so the other must be wrong.

Faith ought to assist us in living into the mystery of life that binary thinking seeks to squelch. Life isn't a simple either/or but is made up of myriad choices and ways of being.

Our way is not the only right way. Faith should help us step out of the particularities of our own life and see the richness of another's. In this way, we live into the complexities of life with a sense of wonder and wholeness.

Some churches, instead of helping people live with ambiguity, foster a sense of uncritical certainty to offset a quickly changing world. I have seen more than one church community pull their doors shut instead of opening themselves up to a changing neighborhood that might challenge their notion of who they are and who God is calling them to be. They cling to memories of their more homogenous history instead of entering into an unknown future. By choosing not to be open to God's future that can be revealed by new relationships, the congregation begins to die.

One year, I was invited to help with a San Francisco church that was down to eight worshiping members. The congregation had had a strong history of mission and justice work around the world, but had done little to engage the neighborhood they were in. Even though their numbers had dwindled and made their future uncertain, they clung to an understanding of who they were instead of who God might be calling them to be. My task was to either assist in the church's revitalization or help it have a good death. I hired four seminary students to work at the church. The church would be a place for them to study and learn. It seemed like such a great idea: What church wouldn't want four young people who were excited about ministry to be in ministry with them? But it was clear from the beginning that the church had no interest in exploring possibilities for their future.

I was not going to be present on Sundays, since I still had a full-time church in another part of San Francisco, but during the summer, I rearranged my Sunday schedule in order to work with the new congregation to prepare to receive the four interns in the fall. On my first Sunday, there were seven people in the congregation—six congregants and the Rev. Jane Schlager, my district superintendent. The church was so hostile toward change that when it was time for Communion, only one person came forward to receive the bread and drink from the cup—the district superintendent.

When the planes hit the Twin Towers on 9/11, I asked the students to go to the church and open the doors wide so people in the neighborhood could enter for prayer and community. Before they could do that, however, they had to find a hammer. The front doors of the church had been nailed shut! The "regulars" knew how to find an open side door and make their way through a maze of hallways to get to the sanctuary. They couldn't imagine that there were people literally outside the doors of their church looking for a spiritual home.

With a faith that didn't allow for the uncertainty ahead of them, they refused to enter into relationships with me or the four interns. The church wound up closing.

## THE RISK OF RELATIONSHIP

It can certainly be scary to open ourselves up to people who might challenge our way of being. Relationships have the power to break through the walls we build and misconceptions we hold. When I began as the bishop of the Mountain Sky Area, which includes churches in Montana, Wyoming, Utah, Colorado, and one church in Idaho, I knew that in order to lead effectively, I had to visit churches. I had to learn from the clergy and laity about the struggles and celebrations of their church's ministries before I could lead them. The first four months of my tenure in the Mountain Sky Area were spent traveling with each of the district superintendents through their districts. It was a grueling schedule as we covered the 470,000 square miles of this area, but it was necessary if I was to get a clear picture of the state of United Methodism in the Mountain Sky Area.

I loved these visits. Folks were proud of their churches, and I was moved by the creative ways they were responding to the hurts and needs in their towns and villages, sharing the love of Christ through acts of compassion and justice. There was great joy in these meetings, and laughter was not in short supply. Some of these churches were in remote areas, and people wept as I crossed the threshold into their church—no one had any memory of a bishop visiting them.

There was another reason why I made these trips. As the first openly lesbian bishop, I knew people had to meet me. In many small communities, LGBTQ people are rare—most leave as soon as they can to move to cities where they can find community with others like them. People had an understanding of what they thought an LGBTQ person was like, but not necessarily from a first-hand encounter. Much had been written about me, from both progressives and conservatives. I wanted people to get to know me personally, for relationships to develop so that we could get beyond the sensationalism of my episcopacy and dig into the work of ministry.

Robin frequently made these trips with me. As a deaconess (a lay order of ministry in The United Methodist Church), she too was interested in seeing these churches. As my spouse, we knew it was important for people to see us together. For many in these small towns, we would be the first married lesbian couple they had ever met. We wanted to dispel any misconceptions about who we were, and to stand authentically and vulnerably before them. In most cases, meeting us was a positive step toward understanding, but that kind of vulnerability always carries the risk of rejection and hurt.

Some of us at Glide took that risk when we bridged a global divide and deepened our relationship with a children's learning center in Kenya after two church members, Travis Woodard and Craig Wood, returned from visiting a niece who was doing an internship there through American University. The learning center serves street children and those impacted by HIV/AIDS in Kawangware, one of the largest Nairobi slums. Most of the inhabitants live on less than $1 a day. Electricity is intermittent, and clean water is in short supply. The couple was so moved by what they saw, they came to my office as soon as they returned to the United States and asked if we could take up a collection for the school. Glide's praxis of ministry, however, is not just about giving money out, but about building relationships that change us all. As a result of Craig and Travis's visit, we started sending a team from Glide to the learning center every eighteen months to learn from and work alongside Kenyan teachers Martha and Charles. Over the years, we watched children grow and were able to sponsor some of them to secondary schools.

There was much sharing between us and our new Kenyan friends. They taught us Swahili, introduced us to Kenyan food, and invited us into their lives. We went on rounds with Majida, the community health worker based at the learning center, seeing where many of the students lived. Stepping over sewage ditches and garbage dumps and steering clear of goats and dogs, we made our way through the alleyways of the slum. The homes were usually a twelve-foot by twelve-foot room made out of corrugated metal, often housing seven people or more. As we listened and learned from lives so different from our own, we had to throw out all assumptions of what made life "rich," "full," and "good." It was tempting to impose our US values and assume we knew what these new friends needed. Over and over again we had to remind ourselves that we were building relationships, not trying to "fix" what we perceived as broken.

But while Martha, Charles, and the children shared their lives so freely with us, many of us held ourselves back. Most of the teams we brought to Kenya had many LGBTQ members. Because homosexuality is criminalized in Kenya and public opinion regarding homosexuality is extremely negative (a Pew research study showed that out of forty-seven countries, Kenya has one of the highest rates of anti-LGBTQ attitudes, with 96 percent of the population believing homosexuality should be rejected[1]), we did not share fully about our own lives. We were careful about the pronouns we used when discussing the people we called "family." Lesbian and gay couples who traveled with us were cautious about how close they stood to their beloved, lest people detect a familiarity and intimacy usually reserved for husband and wife. One time, we met with an underground LGBTQ rights organization; they closed all the windows in the room so people couldn't tell what group was meeting.

We did, however, connect on Facebook, allowing our Kenyan friends a look into our lives. They saw the people we lived with. They saw the causes we supported. They saw pictures of LGBTQ Pride parades. Martha finally asked one of our team members, "Is everyone from Glide gay?" This view into our daily lives, coupled with the care and love we brought into our relationship with Martha, Charles, and the children, caused a change in attitude.

When Robin and I got married and pictures of our wedding day were posted on Facebook, Martha wrote, "Congratulations! I love these ladies."

That experience showed me the potential of Facebook to bring people closer and foster relationships between different kinds of people. But the 2016 elections made clear that social media can also be a polarizing force, where dialogue is replaced by diatribe. Reading through posts on various denominational pages, I am amazed at how dismissive many are of opinions that differ from their own. It is one thing to disagree. It is another to reject the possibility that another's opinion is just as valid as one's own. The lack of civility and respect is beyond the pale. We have also learned how Facebook and other social media platforms have been used by trolls with the expressed intent of creating division and spreading mistruths. A tool that at one time showed so much promise as a way to unite us across our lines of difference by allowing us to see each other's daily lives through words and pictures is now dividing us further. If this instant look into each other's lives is no longer expanding our world so that we can learn how to live with the ambiguity that differences often bring, where can we learn how to do it?

## FAITH AND QUESTIONS

One of my biggest hopes for faith communities is that they would be places that help us live more fully with the complexities of life as revealed in all our lives. The problem is that for many of us, faith development stopped once we were confirmed or graduated from high school. As a result, it cannot help us face the challenges of adulthood. It fails to provide the spiritual resources to live into much of the mystery that is present in our daily living.

James Fowler was a professor of theology and human development at Emory University. I often refer to his "stages of faith,"[2] outlined in his book by the same name, as a way to understand the dynamics at work in the life of congregations, as well as to guide me as I guide others in their own spiritual growth. For Fowler, faith is how we make meaning in our lives. He delineates six stages of faith development, beginning at stage one (which he calls the intuitive-projective faith) when fantasy and reality are often merged, to stage six (the universalizing faith), when people experience a oneness with the Divine and those around them and seek to live a life of service to a greater good.

According to Fowler, stage six is seldom reached, quite possibly because it is preceded by stage five, the "conjunctive faith." This stage rarely is achieved before midlife. It requires one to be aware of the limits of one's own logic and begin to accept that there can be multiple truths, even within the same sacred story. Stage five invites us to lean into ambiguity.

Faith doesn't provide us with easy black-and-white answers but enables us to cope with the discomfort of ambiguity, stretching ourselves beyond our comfort zone as we learn of lives and truths that are different from our own. Jesus invites us to live into this ambiguity over and over again. Have you noticed how Jesus often never directly answered a question, but returned a question with another question? In fact, Jesus answered far fewer questions than he asked!

He wasn't skirting the truth. He was inviting his questioners into the complexities of a life well-lived. In Mark 3:1–6, Jesus enters a synagogue where there is a man with a withered hand. The religious leaders want to catch him in the act of breaking Sabbath rules. Jesus knew that the religious leaders were clinging to the black and white of acceptable behavior for the Sabbath, so he challenges them to live into the gray area: "Is it lawful to do good or to do harm on the Sabbath, to save life or to kill?" Jesus is pressing them to see how rules can actually limit us from engaging in right action. He shows how the spirit of all laws ought to be life-giving. The religious leaders, however, want none of it. They are unmoved by the opportunity to free a man from an infirmity. The New Revised Standard Version says that Jesus was angered by "their hardness of heart."

As a lesbian bishop, my presence creates cognitive dissonance in people: Rules were broken! At the same time, could this be a good and new thing that God is doing? Many people have voiced a fear of meeting me, because it would challenge their belief that an LGBTQ person cannot be a faithful servant of God. The word throughout the area I serve is, "I don't want to meet the new bishop, because I am afraid I might like her!" And what if they did? The inner conflict of beliefs and experience might be unsettling to the comfortable certainty they once felt.

During my visits to churches in my episcopal area, I usually gave a brief devotion in between the two questions I asked each congregation about their ministry and how I could help. Using Matthew 5 and Jesus' instructions to let our lights shine, I included in one of my devotions a story about a teenager at Glide. Each Sunday, Todd would be sitting on the chancel steps, dressed in a wrinkled dress shirt and tie. I imagined that after church he would tear off the shirt and throw it in a corner of his bedroom where it would lie until the following Sunday, when he would put it back on.

He told me his name was Todd, but I am not sure if that really was his name, because Todd was a runaway. The people who were supposed to care for, nurture, and protect him couldn't or wouldn't do that, and the streets were safer than his childhood home. So there was no bedroom corner for Todd to throw his shirt. Each Sunday after church, it was stuffed in the bottom of his backpack, where it remained during the week.

The Glide community tried to look out for Todd. Teri, a recovery group leader who knew something about living on the streets, kept in close contact with Todd. Other members of the church tutored him weekly, so he could keep up with his education. But one Sunday, Todd was absent. The next week and for several weeks after, I would scan the congregation for a sign of Todd, but he was missing.

This worried so many of us. We knew what could happen to a young person on the streets. We knew what a young person who lived on the streets had to do to survive. We did all we could to try to find him, but we always came up empty.

One day, I looked down at the chancel steps, and there in his crumpled dress shirt and tie was Todd! I couldn't wait for the Celebration to be over so I could speak with him. "Todd! Where have you been? I've missed you!" I said, giving him a hug. He stepped back like I had struck him, and his eyes began to water. "You missed me? No one ever noticed when I was gone, ever."

A few weeks later it was his fifteenth birthday. I couldn't imagine having a fifteenth birthday without family. Every birthday celebration in my family home meant a special birthday dinner, cake, and gifts. At one point during the Sunday Celebration, I invited Todd to stand with me. With him by my side, I told the congregation, "Today is Todd's birthday. Let's sing 'Happy Birthday' to him." I knew this congregation well. They were not just going to get through the words of this age-old birthday song. They were going to sing it as a love song to him.

They did not disappoint.

The congregation offered more than just words to Todd. They let their lights shine bright, illuminating the dark places of Todd's heart, literally pouring love from the pews to where he stood, and I watched as that love touched him and changed him. From an initial slouched stance, head bent, with his hair covering his face, Todd transformed before my eyes. He began to pull back his shoulders and stand a little taller. He brought his hands to his face and parted the hair that hung there. He drank in the sight of one thousand people singing to him. As he opened himself to the love that was being offered, I witnessed a miracle. A light that had been long extinguished (if it had ever been lit) suddenly burst forth from Todd's chest, sending love back to the congregation. "Let your light shine," Jesus said (Matt. 5:16). When we love one another, love spills in and out of our lives in healing ways.

I told this story at many of the churches I visited. At one church, a man sat up in one of the front rows. I could tell by his posture and the way he averted his eyes from mine that he was not happy I was there. When I finished my story, he said, "Like you, I love the church. But you need to know: You dimmed my light."

I challenged his notion of rules, of right and wrong. It brought into question his own reading of the Bible and made him less confident in the faith he held. For him and many others, my presence as their episcopal leader was an affront to what they knew to be true. There was no room that another truth might also exist. The question is, can they co-exist?

Since we've been trained to think in binary terms of duality—either/or; right/left; yes/no; true/false; black/white—there is no room for gray, for the fact that truth may be less either/or and more both/and.

Faith is not about certainty. It is about living into the questions and being surprised at where the questions take us. Our presence in each other's lives is an invitation to grow as we encounter more of God's world through the gifts we bring each other through our differences.

As Catholic author Richard Rohr writes,

> In general, we can see that Jesus' style is almost exactly the opposite of modern televangelism or even the mainline church approach of "Dear Abby" bits of inspiring advice and workable solutions for daily living. Jesus is too much the Jewish prophet to merely stabilize the status quo with platitudes.[3]

## STEPPING INTO THE GRAY

In my own life, spiritual growth occurred when I engaged the demands of the gospel more deeply. And it did rattle the status quo of my life. I remember when, during my first appointment to a church in rural New York, Bishop C. Dale White called on the pastors of the conference to join him in an act of civil disobedience in New York City to protest apartheid. I thought apartheid was wrong, and had even preached about it, but now the bishop was calling on me to take a step for which I was not ready. How could I break the law? There are ways to voice our disagreements with policies and injustice. Isn't that enough? Shouldn't we let politicians and processes help create social change?

I didn't go to New York City for the action. Years later, as my spiritual life continued to deepen and grow, I was again invited to engage in civil disobedience and risk arrest. The request this time came from a nun in San Francisco. I had already been serving in the city for several years and had seen how the economy, high housing costs, and broken social systems had created a growth in the homeless population within the city. The Presidio, a military base at the entrance to the Golden Gate, was being decommissioned and turned into a national park. Within the Presidio was a large housing stock where military personnel and their families had lived. The religious community was seeking to use a small portion of that to house the homeless through supportive housing.

Public officials were lobbied, but to no avail. Some said the housing would be demolished. Others saw that the market rate for rentals in San Francisco could help fund the new park. Feeling as if there were no other options than direct action, Sister Bernie, who was the executive director of Religious Witness with Homeless Persons, asked religious leaders in the city to join her in an act of trespassing in order to highlight the housing possibility. I had been serving on the board of Religious Witness. I was a part of the relationships Sister Bernie built with clergy throughout the interfaith community as well as with people living on the streets. Sister Bernie was the connector for many of us, helping homelessness not be just a political issue to be argued about, but providing an awareness that it was about people who had nothing but the streets to call their home.

I responded differently to her call than I did to Bishop White's. I knew I had to participate in this act of civil disobedience. I joined the many clergy and laity of San Francisco, along with community housing advocates and homeless people, in a march through the Presidio. I marched alongside my friend, Lutheran pastor Jeff Johnson. He had never been arrested before either and was as nervous as I was. We marched, sang, and prayed at a rally in front of the housing units. Sister Bernie disappeared for a couple of minutes behind one of the housing units, and then emerged from the front door. "C'mon in," she said, inviting us to trespass onto federal property.

I vividly remember standing at the threshold of the door with Jeff. My stomach was in my throat. *I was about to break the law!* Then, the words to a Robert J. Dufford song rang in my ears, "Be not afraid, I go before you always. Come, follow me, and I will give you rest."[4] With that assurance, Jeff and I looked each other in the eye, joined our hands together, and stepped over the threshold into certain arrest.

Over the years I have reflected on why, in one instance, I couldn't fathom breaking a law and yet a few years later, I could and did. What was different? It wasn't a difference in my sense of justice. I knew apartheid was a sinful social structure that had to end. Why was I able to put my body on the line for one issue but not the other?

I realized it was due to changes in my spiritual life, my engagement with Scripture, and my relationship with Jesus. Jesus shook up the status quo of my life and called me to live into the ambiguity that is created in the tension that occurs when laws fail to serve us and the most vulnerable among us. My faithful response was not predicated by a binary that said *law = right* and *civil disobedience = wrong*. My action was instead being informed by the suffering of others whose lives were unlike mine. My spiritual development had led me to a new place. It was not always comfortable (being arrested never is), but it made my life far richer because it was filled with nuances created by differences.

Perhaps my biggest lessons about living in the gray area of ambiguity were taught by the Glide community. The life experiences of so many of the community members were so unlike my own: drug and alcohol addiction, life on the streets, the oppressive weight of racism, time spent in prison . . . By keeping myself open to those I pastored, not trying to make my experience the "normal" one but one experience of many, my life became immeasurably enriched by those who lived their lives authentically and vulnerably.

It was from those with mental illness that I learned that leaning into ambiguity allows me to respect people whose lived experiences are far from mine and out of my comfort zone. One day, Glide's associate pastor, the Rev. Theon Johnson III, was still getting oriented to his appointment at the church. I had already been there several years and was introducing him to members of the community. One community member came up to us quite agitated. "Pastors!" he said, "I just don't know what to do! My cousin Barack is being inaugurated next weekend, and I am wondering if I should go to Washington, DC, to see him. I mean, he is going to be the new president of the United States!" Theon looked at him, wide-eyed. The man barely took a breath as he was speaking excitedly, "But then again, my other cousin, Ed, has his inauguration as mayor of San Francisco the same day. Can you pray for me, pastors? I just don't know what to do."

The man moved on. Theon was speechless for a moment. "Is this true?" he finally stammered out. I replied, "I don't know if it's true, but he thinks it's true, and that's what counts."

I don't know where my reply came from. I want to think it was a Holy Spirit moment, because my own response gave me pause: what mattered was that *he* thought it was true. Whether it was true or false, my first engagement with him meant stepping into the gray area of his truth. It is from that starting point that relationships deepen, and a fuller truth emerges.

We can mistrust the truth of another's life, experience, and understandings. If it doesn't match our own, we assume it is "less than" or invalid. It is our discomfort with ambiguity that compels us to write off what another says. Instead of being willing to enter into the ambiguity that something might be true for another, we shut ourselves off from another's reality.

One time at Glide, we realized it was a community member's birthday. It was a major cause for celebration because there were times when we weren't sure if John would actually get to see a new year. His addictions and demons often got the best of him. When we realized it was his birthday, we knew we needed to mark the occasion with a cake. I was too busy to get to a bakery, so I turned to Erma Jo. Erma Jo was a part of our recovery circle, fighting her own addictions. She would be clean for a couple of months, and then would slip back into her habit. I would see her lying down on the sidewalk, in a drug-induced stupor. I pulled $20 from my pocket and asked Erma Jo if she could go pick up a cake for John. She nodded and said she would be right back.

Fifteen minutes passed. Then thirty. Then forty-five. It was clear that Erma Jo was not coming back. It didn't take me long to connect the dots: with $20 Erma Jo could hit the streets and buy her next high. Should I have given her the $20 in the first place? Some would respond that I should have known better—"give an addict some money and it will just be used for drugs." But I chose to live in the gray area. I chose to give her the money as a way to respect her place within our community. I saw her as a contributor to our community, even when her addictions sabotaged her personal choices.

It is not always easy to lean into ambiguity. It can be confusing and disappointing. But ultimately, for me, it is an immeasurably more grace-filled way to live. The Holy Spirit is not confined to nor bound up in legalistic thinking. The grace of God flows in unpredictable ways. We are called to follow. We might not know the destination. We might be disappointed when those around us refuse to engage us as we think they ought. Everything we know might be called into question. But still, through it all, there is a "love that will not let us go" that enables us to walk in a world that is unpredictable and confusing.

Author Anne Lamott reflects,

> I have a lot of faith. But I am also afraid a lot, and have no real certainty about anything. I remembered something Father Tom had told me—that the opposite of faith is not doubt, but certainty. Certainty is missing the point entirely. Faith includes noticing the mess, the emptiness and discomfort, and letting it be there until some light returns.[5]

Through all the responses to my election as bishop, I have been pondering this quote. I have asked myself, "Where has my certainty caused me to stray from faith? Have I been willing to engage in the hard questions regarding my own understandings as I expect others whose views are different from mine? Am I willing to wade into the troubled waters of our beloved church and be open to and surprised by the Spirit's work?"

## REMAINING TOGETHER, EVEN IN UNCERTAINTY

I have received mail from people who are angry with my election and encourage me to quit. They point to certain Bible verses and don't desire to engage in conversation. However, I have received far more notes from people who have asked me why I couldn't have waited to become a bishop until after the church changes the rules. I am fascinated by this question. First, there is an acknowledgment of my call to the episcopacy, and an expectation that the church is going to change the restrictions around LGBTQ persons serving as clergy. What is clear to them is that a rule was broken that shouldn't have been, even if the person was called by God. "Couldn't you have just waited?"

In the same way, I am clear that this rule against LGBTQ clergy fails to take seriously the spirituality of LGBTQ United Methodists as children of God. It is cruel in its denial of God's call in the lives of LGBTQ persons. It ultimately harms the body of Christ.

My questioners and I are all certain of our positions.

I wonder, however: "What if our certainty is preventing us from not only living fully into our faith, but also from recognizing how others are living into theirs as well?"

I ask myself: "What if I've been reading the Bible wrong? What if God really abhors homosexuality? What if it is a sin that automatically excludes one from participating in the life and ministry of the church? What if the loving relationships of gay men and lesbians are not reflections of God's love?"

Now, to those who hold a view of homosexuality that is more restrictive than mine, they, too, must ask themselves some questions: "What if I've been reading the Bible wrong? What if homosexuality is one more example of God's creativity? What if homosexuality, like heterosexuality, really is a sacred gift, and those who are gay or lesbian are equal partners in creating God's Beloved Community? What if loving relationships of gay men and lesbians are a reflection of God's love?"

If I am wrong, what has been the cost in welcoming gay men and lesbians to the table as equal partners with straight men and women? How have I failed as a follower of Jesus?

If nothing else, by welcoming LGBTQ persons to the faith community, I have offered a group of people that have been kept at the margins a chance to experience the love of God. In addition, the church has benefited from the gifts of those who have participated openly in the life of the church. (Let's be clear: The church has benefited, is benefiting, and always will benefit from the service of LGBTQ persons who are called to make The United Methodist Church their spiritual home. No amount of legislation will prevent the Spirit from calling people—including LGBTQ persons—to ministry within our church.)

However, for those who currently seek to maintain the restrictive policies regarding homosexuality and The United Methodist Church, what if they are wrong? What has been the cost in excluding gay men and lesbians from full participation in the body of Christ as found in the UMC? What have we lost? What has it done to the souls of LGBTQ persons, and their own?

I, for one, would rather be faulted for erring on the side of grace.

Though I've spoken repeatedly about the need to move away from black-and-white binaries into the ambiguous "gray," I realize I am using an incorrect metaphor.

Leaning into ambiguity is not about living in the gray areas of life. Quite the opposite. When we lean into ambiguity, we throw out our black and white crayons and open up a box filled with a wild array of colors. Each color has its unique hue and adds to the palette of life.

There are no clear lines to color inside (or outside). We are invited to enjoy how the colors stand out as well as blend together. It is messy and at times chaotic, but it is so very rich. This is something I learned at Glide. The great diversity found at the church—whether race, class, sexual orientation, gender identity, or religious belief (or no belief)—meant there was no "typical" Glide member. Each person was invited to be fully themselves through the giving and receiving of unconditional love and unconditional acceptance. It was a beautiful thing to behold, as people thrived in this environment. People who had fled oppressive churches or small towns, who had known much bullying as children because others sensed they were "different," who were taught to hate themselves, blossomed joyously into their unique selves. We weren't all alike. We didn't agree on everything. The ways we engaged with the world (and the world engaged with us) were not the same at all. But together, life was bigger, the colors bolder, and the love deeper than I have ever experienced.

Every Sunday, on our drive home, Robin and I would look at each other wide-eyed and say, "How blessed are we to be in community with people so different from us."

Lean into ambiguity and live into the full colors of life!

Chapter 4

# DIVERSITY IS A SIGN
# OF DIVINITY

Robin and I met while working at a junior high church camp
in the early 1990s. We both had volunteered a week of our
time, Robin as the camp nurse and I as the program director. We loved that week, high in the mountains, surrounding
young people with the love of God. We also loved that we
got to hike each day through the glorious Sierra Mountains.
We volunteered for many summers after that, and that annual
week at camp was one of the highlights of each year.

Recognizing in each other a fellow hiker, we began to
add on a week of our own camping right after the conclusion
of the church camp. We would travel to Lassen Volcanic
National Park in Northern California. Mount Lassen marks
the start of the Cascade Range, which runs from Northern
California into British Columbia. That region is recogniz-
able from the air by the dormant (and not so dormant) vol-
canos that run the length of the mountain range. Mount
Lassen itself last erupted in 1917, and the landscape of the
park is otherworldly—lava flows, bubbling mudpots, and
boiling lakes are scattered throughout the park as the ter-
rain displays various stages of recovery from the eruption.

While Robin and I love to hike and try to hike as
often as we can, we haven't been lured to become birders.
Friends we hike with can point out the different species of
birds by their size, color, and song, while we just call them

"colorful" or "pretty." Being such big aficionados of Lassen, we decided we would at least learn the flora even if we were never going to learn the fauna. Each year, we grabbed our books on the flowers and trees of Lassen and tried to relearn all that we had forgotten since we last visited.

As we hiked, we would stop with a book and feel the stem of a flower. Is it square? Then it must be in the mint family, most likely coyote mint. We would notice the common California astor and mountain cinquefoil. As we ascended higher and higher on the trails, pussy-paws would line the hiking path, and there would be a whole new set of wildflowers to learn.

Standing atop one of the peaks within the park, one could spy Mount Shasta to the north, the Sierra Nevadas to the south, the high Nevada desert to the west, and the fertile valley as well as the coastal range to the east. It is a beautiful wonder to behold, leaving me breathless as I ponder God's creation. How could one doubt the existence of God while standing on top of the world? The landscape shows an intricate connection, as one geological zone connects to the next.

Why could we not remember the flowers in a landscape we loved so much? What was it about the biodiversity that baffled two relatively well-educated women each year and sent us back cramming with our "flowers of Lassen" books? Could it be that in spite of the fact that diversity is a necessary and beautiful part of creation, it is too great for our minds to comprehend?

## THE CHALLENGE OF HUMAN DIVERSITY

Our hikes on Lassen were not the only time I have had trouble taking in diversity. After twelve years of serving Bethany

United Methodist Church, I remember the panic I felt when I became associate dean of academic affairs at Pacific School of Religion. When I left Bethany, I had spent a third of my life with that community. After becoming intricately entwined in the lives of those I shared ministry with at Bethany, I found it daunting to consider learning the names of the faculty, staff, and students of a relatively small school. I remember thinking, "I will never learn all these names and keep the records of the students in order." Confusion began to turn to fear.

The good news was that I was able to learn the names of those in this new community, but I will never forget the feelings of panic and inadequacy I had when I stepped onto the campus to begin my new job. What made the difference? What enabled me to move past the fear and discover that I could not only learn the names of all those on campus, but also delight in this new group of people? I decided the only way to get over my fear was to throw my whole self into the community, learning not only names, but also the stories of those who were around me.

This lesson helped me as I began my ministry at Glide. The Glide community, with tens of thousands of radically diverse members, constituents, and supporters, could have been my undoing, overwhelming me by the new and varied people in my care. Thanks to the lesson I learned at the seminary, I brought my whole self to Glide. But it wasn't a one-way sharing. By staying open to lives that were so different from mine, I found beauty in the most unexpected places and people.

There was a saying that guided community life at Glide: "We all are in recovery from something." That became the great equalizer, for it is not just drugs and alcohol that enslave us. There is something each one of us battles that keeps us from being our full selves, addictions that sabotage us over and over again. Whether food, shopping, ego, drugs, or alcohol, when we join together and support each other in the recovery process, we find strength in unlikely places and people.

Teri was a long-time Glide member. Teri was the first truly two-spirited person[1] I had ever met. During the week, Teri presented as male. There was no mistaking him. But on weekends, Teri presented as female, fully embracing her feminine side.

Teri left home at an early age. Sexual orientation and gender identity issues made Teri an outcast even in their own family, while being a black person in US culture made Teri feel as if the whole world was against them. Many years on the streets, jail time, and drug use had eroded Teri's sense of self-worth. Glide's recovery program helped Teri face their demons and begin to reclaim who they were as well as develop into a leader at Glide.

Teri came to my office one day and named a major gap in our ministry. Glide Sunday Celebrations were powerful experiences. Undergirded by the moving music ministry of the Glide Ensemble, Celebrations filled people in places they didn't even realize were empty. Many wandered into Glide to hear the music. The sanctuary was filled with the "Nones" (those with no previous church experience) and the "Dones" (those who, for a number of reasons, left the church). For some, just crossing the threshold was difficult because it brought up painful wounds from previous church experiences. Celebrations were high energy and emotional. Ushers knew to keep a box of tissues handy and would often be seen moving up and down the aisles, passing them down the pews to weeping worshipers. Teri, from their perch in the choir, could see the people's emotional responses to Celebration, and came to see me one day.

"Pastor, we need to do something for all those folks on Sunday morning that have been broken open by the Spirit but have no place to talk about what happened to them." Teri suggested a recovery circle. Recovery circles were held throughout the week at Glide, but not on weekends. Teri both noted the need for this kind of support by those already in recovery, but also for those whose experience at Celebration left them raw and vulnerable, elated and filled with love. A Sunday recovery circle could be the place they could come to process what they experienced.

Since Teri had had so much experience in Glide's recovery program, I invited them to be the Sunday recovery facilitator. Each week, the two of us met for an hour to discuss both the group dynamics and Teri's own recovery. We couldn't have been more different in terms of our life experiences. Our meetings were sometimes weepy, sometimes fiery, but always honest as we brought our full selves to our time together. Even though we may have been at the same Sunday gathering, due to our differences in background and social location, the lens we brought to it was vastly dissimilar, so the takeaways, insights, and questions we had were very different. We had to learn how to see these differences as gifts that could offer us even greater wisdom than as things to discount. We began to see one another as providing an important window through which to encounter the world. Both our worlds became enlarged through our relationship with one another. Each week was a time for us to stand on holy ground together and discover that through the diversity we brought to one another's lives, we gained a fuller sense of divinity.

After becoming pastor at Glide, I often forgot about the confusion and fear I experienced when I stepped onto the Pacific School of Religion campus. When friends visited from less diverse communities, I was always surprised by their initial emotions as they stepped into the Glide sanctuary: "Will I be safe?" I saw the fear and suspicion as they rubbed elbows with people who were not only strangers, but, to them, strange.

Why is it that often a first response to diversity is fear rather than curiosity?

I have seen fear and mistrust win over curiosity and wonder over and over again when someone is faced with something or someone new or different. There are times when I have shut myself down instead of opening myself up to experience the new and unusual. It is only much later that I realize I have caused myself to miss out on something wonderful and life-giving.

## GOD'S CREATIVITY

The creation stories in the Hebrew Scriptures reveal a God intent on creating a world filled with difference: earth and heaven and water; animals on the land, fish in the sea, and birds in the air. To all this, God affirmed, "It is good." God didn't create one animal, one kind of fish or bird, but revealed God's infinite imagination through the myriad types of living creatures. Animals could be as diverse as giraffes and starfish and everything in between. Birds of a feather may flock together, but the diversity within birds makes for many different flocks (and while I can't name them, I have friends who can).

While we can recognize God's creativity in the species around us, what makes it difficult for us to comprehend diversity among the human species? Could it be that we read the story of Adam and Eve so literally that we narrow our understanding of humankind?

Often, those who hold anti-LGBTQ views will say that "God made Adam and Eve, not Adam and Steve." Actually, God made Adam and Eve as well as Adam and Steve. God even made those who, as they come into the fullness of their identity, were once Eve but now are Adam. I believe that Adam and Eve's story holds a clue to our aversion to diversity—but names and genders have nothing to do with it.

Adam and Eve were given a beautiful garden to live in. All the varieties of birds, animals, and yes, even flowers, were given by God for humanity to delight in. God placed it all before Adam and Eve—all the different species were there for them to enjoy. Genesis 2 says that Adam named all the creatures that God had created. By naming them, Adam took notice of each one of them. Each was special because it was different from the rest. All were a reflection of God's creativity, given to Adam and Eve for their sustenance and enjoyment.

Except for one.

There was one tree that God warned Adam and Eve not to touch. While they had free range on all of creation, God warned them not to eat from the tree of the knowledge of good and evil. In fact, God's words were like a "Danger, Poison!" label: Do not eat from this tree or you will *die*!

But the serpent came along and challenged what God had told them: "You won't die. In fact, you will know everything going on."

The story tells us:

So when the woman saw that the tree was good for food, and that it was a delight to the eyes, and that the tree was to be desired to make one wise, she took of its fruit and ate; and she also gave some to her husband, who was with her, and he ate. Then the eyes of both were opened, and they knew that they were naked; and they sewed fig leaves together and made loincloths for themselves.

(Gen. 3:6–7)

Here is what is fascinating in the story: in spite of what God had warned them, they didn't die. But their naiveté did. Suddenly Adam and Eve knew things and felt things they hadn't before.

The original enjoyment of creation turns to fear and suspicion. Even their nakedness, once something that was so organic as it enfleshed them with the created world, becomes shameful. As they hide their nakedness from each other, their eyes can no longer take in the beauty of God's diverse creation. By eating from the tree of the knowledge of good and evil, Adam and Eve have broken connection with creation. Through this broken relationship, the entire world, as well as we ourselves, became broken.

The brokenness of the world is hard to face. It is heartbreaking work to hold both good and evil, the beauty and ugliness found in the world. This world will break your heart, over and over again. Your comfort will die, as you find yourself disturbed by injustice. Your privilege might die, as your bubble bursts and you realize that not everyone's life is as easy as yours. Embracing that awareness would require you to step out, stand up, and shout down the forces of evil and injustice, in all the many forms those forces present themselves.

Is this what causes us to draw back from diversity? Is it too much for our hearts to bear, to see in our differences not only our shared humanity, but the myriad hurts we inflict on each other who are unlike us? Is this how neighbors of Jews were able to avert their eyes as friends were rounded up for the concentration camps? Is this why we pass by people who are holding up a sign asking for food, trying not to think of the supper that is waiting for us at home? Is this the reason why so many whites can deny racism's impact on the lives of people of color? Is this what causes us to draw back and seek comfort in sameness? Is the knowledge of good and evil too much for us to comprehend, so we make our lives small by avoiding diversity?

Perhaps God foresaw our diversity aversion, so wove diversity into the very being of Godself so we would have to continually wrestle with diversity as we grow in our intimacy with God. Through the Trinity, God is three in one. The God in Three Persons expresses difference as an innate part of God's identity. But as Episcopal bishop C. Andrew Doyle challenged us at a United Methodist Council of Bishops meeting, "We don't really believe in the Trinity, otherwise we wouldn't have such a hard time accepting diversity."

God as expressed as Creator, Redeemer, and Sustainer is One yet Three, and is Three yet One. In the Oneness, the distinctiveness of the Three is not watered down, diminished, or denied. In fact, each is enhanced through the unity of the One. God, by revealing Godself as Three in One, invites us to reclaim the wonder found in the garden of Eden, to delight once again in the diversity of creation.

Is this possible for humankind?

When I was an undergrad at Drew University, there were only two out LGBTQ people in my class of 1980. I think back now and realize how courageous they were, to live such open lives when so many knew no other option but the closet. Robert and Nancy were so patient with the rest of us who saw their gayness as a rare and exotic thing. I loved the gentle challenge Nancy left all of us, as she placed this quote under her senior picture: "Can human beings stand the diversity of their species?" Every time I flip through my yearbook and read her quote, I somberly reflect on the question. There is so much I see that causes me to answer, "No." We cannot stand the diversity of our species. We seem to gravitate to people who are like us. Whether race, class, educational level, political leanings, or religious traditions, we default to creating community with people who are like us.

## LESSONS FROM THE CORPORATE WORLD

When I traded ministry in New York's Catskill Mountains for ministry in San Francisco, I was suddenly confronted with diversity as I had never before experienced it. At Bethany United Methodist Church, a small congregation that averaged less than one hundred people in worship, there were seven different languages spoken. Add to the mix diverse cultures, economic classes, races, sexual orientations, gender identities, abilities, educational levels, and immigration statuses, and this small congregation represented less a melting pot and more a patchwork quilt of varied colors and textures.

The demographics of this small church were not an anomaly in San Francisco. United Methodism was highly diverse in the City by the Bay. Living, working, and worshiping with such diversity isn't easy. Finding our connection, even as United Methodists sharing a common theology and polity, was difficult. There were tensions present even as we experienced a sacredness in our differences. San Francisco United Methodist Missions, a city-wide organization that provided a forum for us to come together in shared ministry, was the place where this tension was often played out. In the mid-1990s, we realized we needed to work on learning to live with each other, with all our differences.

We turned to denominational resources for assistance, hoping to find programs that could help us gain skills and knowledge in cross-cultural sensitivity through diversity training. We were surprised to see how little the church had to offer. While there were language resources for various racial/ethnic churches (like hymnbooks and church leadership guides translated in various languages), there were no resources at that time that brought us together in ways that celebrated rather than diminished our differences.

We searched and searched. We spoke with denominational staff. Nothing was available that could help us navigate the rich diversity found in our area. But there was a place that did offer the resources we were looking for: the business world. Major companies had already discovered that by offering trainings on diversity and ensuring that diversity was not only present in the workforce, but celebrated, the work environment improved and creativity and performance were enhanced.

One article on workplace diversity noted:

> Co-workers with diverse cultural backgrounds bring unique experiences and perceptions to the table in groups and work teams. Pooling the diverse knowledge and skills of culturally distinct workers together can benefit companies by strengthening teams' productivity and responsiveness to changing conditions.

Each employee in a diverse workplace possesses unique strengths and weaknesses derived from their culture in addition to their individuality. When managed properly, diversity in the workplace can leverage the strengths and complement the weaknesses of each worker to make the impact of the workforce greater than the sum of its parts.[2]

There is a richness in community when diverse experiences are pooled. Skills are broadened. Collaboration has greater depth and brings possibilities that more homogenous communities cannot easily (if at all) attain. Matthew Yglesias wisely stated, "Nobody knows everything, and no group of people knows everything. But a peculiar attribute of homogeneous groups is that they can be unusually *blind to what they don't know*."[3]

This was certainly true for me as I worked with Teri. I would have stayed woefully ignorant of the challenges so many in the Glide community face if I had not developed a pastoral relationship with Teri. I would have been less a preacher, pastor, and person if I had kept Teri at arm's length or if either of us had refrained from intentionally getting to know each other.

Why do we in the church have such a hard time with the concept that diversity is not only a good thing, but it is also required of us? It has been more than fifty years since Martin Luther King Jr. noted that the most segregated hour in the United States is Sunday at 11 a.m. How has our lack of diversity hampered both the ability to deepen the spirituality that we offer each other as well as the witness we offer to the world? Businesses have come to see that the diversity of their workforce assists them in connecting their product to the community around them:

To be profitable in a diverse, globalized marketplace, savvy companies are making efforts to look more like the community around them. If you employ only those who identify with a small portion of the market, you just don't have access to the insights, experiences and worldviews of the full marketplace.[4]

When I was growing up on Long Island, a taco from Jack in the Box was considered exotic; now, Mexican food is a staple in every US town and city. In an age when diversity is found in everything from the food we eat to the languages we hear on television, we make the gospel less compelling to our communities when our worship is reduced to a one-size-fits-all offering. When we fail to include others who aren't like us, not only in our pews but also around our leadership tables, we lessen the fullness of life that is offered to us as the body of Christ.

Inviting diversity is hard but necessary work. Neil Lenane, the business leader of talent management at Progressive Insurance, astutely notes that "if you do not intentionally include, you unintentionally exclude."[5] Every community has its diversity, but often it is seldom acknowledged.

I am the bishop over a large area filled with small towns and villages, some isolated by geography, and at first glance it might look like my region is short on diversity. While the 2017 census showed that overall, whites make up 61 percent of the US population, in my region, the nearest state that comes close to that average is Colorado, which is 70 percent white. Wyoming is a whopping 89 percent white![6]

Race is only one aspect of diversity. Educational level, economic class, skills, physical abilities, culture, life experiences, perspectives, and age are just a few of the ways even small towns are diverse. However, we water down differences when we think "everyone looks like us." What would happen, even in a small town and even smaller church, if the diversity that was truly present in the community was not only unmasked but highlighted? How much richer would Sunday morning be if these differences were acknowledged in worship? How would our common life, filled with the true richness of our differences, expand our understanding of God, ministry, and spirituality?

Companies know something churches seem to forget: the potential for greater personal growth increases when people are exposed to differences, and this growth has a positive impact on the overall health of the organization. "Spending time with culturally diverse co-workers can slowly break down the subconscious barriers of ethnocentrism and xenophobia, encouraging employees to be more well-rounded members of society."[7]

Katherine Phillips, professor at Columbia Business School, notes, "Being with similar others leads us to think we all hold the same information and share the same perspective. This perspective, which stopped the all-white groups from effectively processing the information, is what hinders creativity and innovation."[8] What does this mean for the ministries we create in our churches, when we plan them without intentionally seeking diversity in our ministry teams?

Studies show that diverse groups are more creative than more homogenous groups. Bringing together a wide variety of skills, opinions, and life experiences, they are more likely to understand the bigger picture, with its complexities, challenges, and opportunities, and find unusual and inventive ways to address them. Some studies say this is because "the presence of group members unlike oneself causes people to think differently. One study found that 'the mere presence of diversity in a group creates awkwardness, and the need to diffuse this tension leads to better group problem solving.'"[9]

Diversity creates healthy communities. However, in the United States, segregation is increasing in some areas, particularly in urban centers. While diversity might be a stated value, studies show that the more affluent people become, the more they gravitate to others who share their economic class. This class bias has a deep impact, creating more homogeneity in communities, which then affects the quality of education, opportunities for advancement, and the overall health of communities.[10]

When a group of Illinois residents were asked in 2016 about the kind of community they would like to live in, individuals of all races indicated that they wanted a diverse community. While people of color actually chose to move into racially diverse neighborhoods, whites chose less diverse neighborhoods.[11]

### THE CHALLENGES OF DIVERSITY

Diversity is not easy to live into. At times, it is difficult because we are often confronted with our own ignorance. Sometimes we are embarrassed or ashamed as we begin to know what we didn't know. Our privilege or lack of privilege often causes us to respond with suspicion to those who are different from us. Sometimes we are afraid of saying the wrong thing and being seen as culturally insensitive. But all relationships have hidden land mines to be navigated and negotiated. What is it about relationships with those who are different from us that make those land mines more frightening to us? At Glide, I stepped in land mines frequently. When I did, I was grateful for the grace others offered me as I continued to open myself up to lives that were so different from my own. I had to acknowledge that my way was not the only way, and frequently admit when I didn't know or understand something. It was humbling and enriching, both at the same time.

When the welcome is wide, you have to be open to everyone and all they bring with them. Meetings at Glide were often wildly chaotic and loud, and seldom followed the flow of the stated agenda. The commitment to diversity meant that every voice had a place at the table. Sometimes someone would get triggered by the topic being discussed or by an individual's actions. The focus of the meeting would take an unexpected turn as a result. Any semblance of a type A personality I might have harbored was quickly jettisoned as I learned to ride the wave of such a dynamic community. It was exhilarating as much as it was exhausting, but it was always a gift as we learned from one another in ways that the agenda never could have allowed if we had dutifully followed it.

Even worship had its challenges. I couldn't assume a common theological language or even sacred text. In the Glide community were Pentecostals and recovering Catholics, as well as Buddhists, Jews, Muslims, agnostics, and atheists. I realized the challenge posed by such a diverse community my first Easter at Glide. I had arrived as pastor about a month earlier and was still learning how to provide spiritual leadership to a community unlike one I had ever pastored.

Easter is awesome at Glide. For a community grounded in recovery, the miracle of resurrection happens all the time, as those who have been deadened due to addictions experience new life in their recovery. The Celebration itself simply soars on the wings of the Spirit, and the power of resurrection is profoundly present.

I was greeting worshipers after the Easter Celebration when one of the regulars came up to speak with me. "That was a great Celebration," he began, "But did you have to speak so much about Christ?" "Um, well, it is Easter," I replied. "Yeah, about that: did you have to go there?"

I have thought about his comments often. He felt the power of Christ that day, even if it wasn't the way he would describe it, or the words he would use. Christian words and symbols had been used to batter and bruise him in the past, and the wounds were still raw. I realized he wasn't the only one. Glide was filled with people for whom the traditional language and rituals of the church did not only leave them indifferent, but actually hampered their relationship with God and others. Paige, one of my seminary interns, described the Glide community in this way: "Glide is a church for people who hate church."

As a preacher, I realized I had to keep my sermons theologically grounded, while using words and new rituals that invited people to a transforming encounter with the Divine. As the Rev. Lloyd Wake, a former Glide pastor, wrote about Celebrations:

> Glide Celebrations . . . have helped to eliminate the chasm between intellect and emotions so that people feel themselves to be whole persons. The artificial barriers between intellect, spirit and body are removed, and spontaneity has been both encouraged and affirmed. Another condition to which the Celebrations respond is the rejection of traditional religious symbols, practices, and values by many, especially young people. Young people have experienced the

oppression of these traditions. At the same time, many have doubts and a sense of despair about the future. Having rejected the past and having no certainty about the future, their overwhelming concern is for the here and now. Personal fulfillment and social goals such as freedom from oppression and a world with peace and justice must be achieved now. Passively waiting for future fulfillment is a copout. Religion must speak and respond to contemporary human conditions. Speculative definitions about God, Christ, heaven, hell and the future are totally irrelevant.[12]

It was people's experience at Celebration that caused change in their lives. Being rigid about the theological terms we used would create a human hindrance to God's movement in the community. My task was to invite them into the story of God's redeeming work in the world and then step aside to make room for the Holy Spirit. When I was able to do this well, I was amazed to see the gospel materialize before my eyes. One day, I was speaking about how there is a wound within all of us that seeks to be healed. Because so many in the community had been harmed by others who had used the Bible as a weapon, I had to find ways to offer the gospel through storytelling. Instead of reading directly from the Bible, I often wove the biblical text into my sermon, grounding it in the realities those in the sanctuary lived. This day, I retold the story of the woman who had been bleeding for twelve years. This had made her an outcast in her community. She was desperate for a healing, and when she heard that Jesus was going to be in her area, she went to find him. She had heard the ways he had healed others, so as Jesus was walking through the crowd of her town, she elbowed her way forward so that she could touch him. She so longed for a healing, but all she could do was reach for the hem of his robe. Jesus felt her touch and told her that because of her faith, she was healed.

As I was preaching, I felt someone caressing my feet. Glide is packed on Sunday mornings. Ushers have to line the aisles with chairs, people sit in the windowsills, and the steps up into the narthex are often filled with children as well as adults. There is always a bustle of activity around me as I preach. I looked down to see if indeed someone was touching me, when I saw a woman in a hospital gown, lovingly rubbing my feet as I preached!

It was Char, a longtime member of Glide. She had been admitted to the psychiatric ward of a hospital but that Sunday walked out the door and straight to Glide. She knew she was still not well, so she went to the place that offered her hope and new life. When she heard the story of the woman who was seeking a healing, she took it to heart. She, too, yearned for healing. For her, the actor in the story was the woman who was like her. It was that nameless woman's desire for healing that mattered, and which she mirrored.

So, without the familiar Christian rituals or symbols, what was it that unified us? What created a community in a place where such broad diversity could have kept us separate from each other? It was the experience of unconditional love and unconditional acceptance that was core to the theology we expressed at Glide. It extended beyond words and theological correctness. This love helped people find a place in community like they had never experienced before. It helped them bring their full selves, in all their glorious uniqueness, to Glide. It helped build relationships and places of connection. It helped us recognize one another as part of the same family.

Too often, we allow our theology to get in the way of our relationships with one another. Instead of seeing our kinship as all being children of God, we allow our theological words and doctrines to divide us. If God is love and love is of God, this should be what unites us in Beloved Community. Instead of widening the circle of community, however, we too often use it as a litmus test to determine who is in and who is out. But love moves beyond human constructs and systems.

Those who have opposed my election and consecration as bishop have used their theological arguments and scriptural interpretation to create a division between themselves and me as well as those who are like me. I, too, however, hold to certain theological arguments and scriptural interpretations that create division. The biggest thing I learned at Glide is that when we put love at the center, we remain in relationship together even when what we think and believe could separate us.

This is our challenge as people of faith in the twenty-first century. While we all hold to the particulars of our faith, which are seen through the lens of our cultural context, love transcends these differences and unites us, speaking a language more powerful than our theological words and definitions. Love helps us live into the diversity found in God's beloved creation—including humankind.

## THE LOVE CONNECTION

Through the experience of unconditional love and unconditional acceptance found at Glide, my own eyes were opened to much I had failed to see. I realized that my class, skin color, and gender caused me to not see some

people. But because *I* was being received with unconditional love and acceptance, I began to walk in the world differently. I no longer averted my eyes from those who were
unlike me. Instead, as I made my way through city streets, I
greeted the people I passed.

My walk from the Powell Street BART (subway)
stop to Glide was not pretty. One must choose one's
steps carefully there, because vomit and even human
excrement are often found on the sidewalks. Against
buildings, men and women are sprawled out, heading up
or coming down from a high. In doorways, people are
asleep on cardboard boxes, their bags of belongings serving as pillows.

I was often eager to leave the Tenderloin neighborhood, where Glide is, to take BART home to Colma, where
we lived. The two areas couldn't be more different: while
the TL, as it is known, is gritty, loud, and all concrete,
Colma, just south of San Francisco, is the only necropolis in
North America, with 1.5 million dead people and 1,500 living residents. Early in San Francisco's development, it was
recognized that as a peninsula that was seven miles by seven
miles, the city would use up land quickly as it expanded.
So the city government decided to ban all future burials.
It bought a section of land, Colma, just beyond the city's
southern border and began exhuming bodies for reburial
in Colma. Currently, there are seventeen cemeteries in
the town (including a pet cemetery where it is rumored
that Tina Turner's dog is buried in one of Turner's fur
coats). Colma's history and service to people at a time of
their greatest need are sources of pride for its residents, but
they are not without a sense of humor. Each new resident is
given a bumper sticker when they move into the town: "It's
great to be ALIVE in Colma."

The BART ride from the TL to Colma was only twenty minutes, but it was like entering another country. Leaving the grit and bustle of the TL, I would ascend the escalator at my station stop and be met with green trees, grass, and lots of flowers in the Catholic cemetery across the street from our home.

After one particularly long day at Glide, I was ready to get home and began to make my way to the BART station. I crossed one of the streets and saw a woman passed out lying in her own urine. I wanted to turn away, but there was something about her that made me keep looking at her. Did I know her?

In one hand, there was a Barbie doll. Barbie's blond hair and elegant dress were in stark contrast to the woman's greasy hair, torn clothes, and dirty hands that held the doll. I had to wonder: Did her mother give her a Barbie when she was younger? Did she have siblings? Perhaps even children of her own?

What pushed her to the streets? Did anyone miss her? Was there someone out there wondering what happened to her, looking for her, searching for her? Was there someone who cared about her, wanting to hold her as tightly as she clung to Barbie? She was someone's daughter, after all.

She *was* someone's daughter.

She was *someone's* daughter.

She was someone's *daughter*.

Then I realized: she and nameless, countless others will take their places on our city sidewalks as long as we think they are of someone else's family. Until we see those on the streets as our kin, people we miss, those we've been searching for, loved ones we long to hold and care for, our streets will remain the address of the forgotten and overlooked.

It was my experience of the unconditional love and acceptance as expressed at Glide that opened my eyes: The woman who held the Barbie doll, tenderly, tightly in her hand I now recognized as my daughter, my sister, my mother. It is love that connects us and changes us, turning strangers into family members we didn't know we were missing.

As I reflect on my own spiritual growth, I realize that my greatest lessons didn't come from seminary classrooms, lectures by brilliant theologians, or even engaging Bible studies. It was my relationships with those who are most different from me, particularly the homeless, that helped me see God's face more clearly. Before I began as pastor at Glide, my commitment to diversity was largely intellectual. While I valued diverse opinions, authors, and people, my world was fairly homogenous. I had mainly white, well-educated, middle-class friends. While my words spoke about a commitment to diversity, the life I led was anything but, much like those Illinois whites in the research discussed earlier, who claimed to want diverse neighborhoods, but chose not to live in them. I was committed to just and fair public policies for homeless people, but I was not in relationship with anyone who was actually homeless. I worked *for* homeless people instead of *with* them. There were regulars on the streets I walked who I would nod to when running errands, but I never stopped to talk with them and get to know their life stories.

There was one man who stood on a street corner day in and day out. He was a large man. His feet were usually wrapped in dirty bandages that oozed blood and pus. He would stand on that street corner and sing the blues like an angel. I encountered him in a deeper way one Sunday afternoon. Sunday afternoon, for pastors, is the time of the week when we—or at least I—am simply good for nothing. By Sunday afternoon, having spent myself in worship, about the only thing I can do is take a nap. I don't want to see anybody, I don't want to talk with anybody . . . Basically I'm not fit for human contact.

One Sunday, I had to go run an errand in the afternoon before crashing on the couch. It was one of those Sunday afternoons when I shouldn't have been out in public. If anyone had come close, I'm sure I would have reflexively responded with a growl. I was walking along the street where the homeless guy was singing. I was exhausted, head down, collar up, and I raised my head and our eyes met. And he looked at me with this big wide grin and said, "Sister, do you have love in your heart?"

I felt like all the air had been pushed out of my lungs and I was in the tightest double bind of my life. Have I got love in my heart? Have I got love in my heart on Sunday afternoon at three o'clock?

I couldn't say no because I knew that wasn't altogether true, but I confess, I didn't want to say yes. I didn't want to say yes because I was afraid of what a yes answer would entail. I was tired and I was cranky, and if I said yes I knew something would be required of me that I simply didn't want to muster the energy to offer. The last thing I wanted to do on a Sunday afternoon between three and four o'clock was to have love obligate me to do anything— because obligation to one another is what love is all about.

We live in an age when love seems in exceedingly short supply. If we have love in our hearts, it means we're going to live in ways that improve not just ourselves but everyone; we are going to make choices mindful of how every choice we make affects everyone else in the world. Every decision we make, whether in the political sphere, the religious sphere, or the personal sphere, ought to be grounded in a sense of our interconnectedness and the fact that when one suffers, we all suffer. Love requires us to remain connected to one another. It means that your life matters to me, I am going to enter into your joy, but I am also going to walk with you when you are hurting the most. And when it gets too hard, I am going to offer to carry you.

Love is hard work, especially in a world that disappoints, in a culture where it's every man, woman, and child for themselves, in times like these, when it's unfashionable to empty one's self for another. The demands of love, what it requires of us, seem too high.

And that's exactly how I felt that Sunday afternoon in San Francisco. The price of love seemed high when it was all that I could do to just walk down the street. Still, that singer of the street's question still nags at me, "Sister, do you have love in your heart?" This love ought to motivate me to break down the arbitrary barriers that we put each other in so that I can encounter others in all their dazzling diversity and beauty. This love I have for myself and my well-being ought to cause me to extend that well-being to others, especially the most vulnerable.

I am going to love you the way I love myself because in the end we all will be changed and we all will be brought to a place of wholeness and healing, of justice and joy. So there I was, facing this question that was posed to me: Sister, do you have love in your heart?

And I finally was able to look that singer in the eye: "Yes, yes, I have love in my heart." And he spread his arms and said, "Then give me a hug."

When we open ourselves to the diversity found in the lives around us, we find ourselves standing on holy ground. We learn that God speaks through those who aren't like us and sometimes provides us with our deepest spiritual lessons. There is nothing to fear as we discover our lives are enriched beyond measure by those we once discounted or ignored. The world becomes even more precious, full of surprises that enrich our lives. Love is let loose in the world. And this love changes everything.

Chapter 5

# UNITY IS NOT UNIFORMITY

When I was in high school, the highlight of the year was the Blue and Gold competition. In this spring event, all the high school girls were divided into two teams representing our school colors. Each team chose a theme to develop a program around. There were several parts to the competition: modern dance, calisthenics, sporting events, modern jazz, and marching. Besides the points distributed for each event, points were also given for music, art, and costumes.

Blue and Gold was a big deal. Friendships were made and lost because of the intensity of the competition—if a good friend was assigned to the opposite team, that friendship took a hiatus. Each team closely guarded its music sets, routines, and costumes, lest the other team find out about a complicated routine or design and try to best it in advance. Competition was fierce.

Ask anyone in my family about my ability to dance and they will tell you, "Grace certainly isn't Karen's middle name." For girls like me, who could never make it on the dance or calisthenics teams, there was marching. Marching meant just that. Think "military drill team." All of us who had two left feet would work for weeks trying to perform our routine with great precision. Knees high, turns crisp, and each member perfectly spaced from the next, we would march to the music of a cassette tape that had several songs of the day edited into one, each musical selection segueing into another as we moved from one part of the routine to the next.

I can remember stepping onto the gym floor in my marching costume as the music began, working hard to remember the routine and being mindful of the rest of my teammates. It was exhilarating to perform the routine as flawlessly as we could. Tension rose toward the end of the evening's competition, as a senior moved to the center of the gym with a blue flag and a gold flag, one team to her right and the other to her left. A hush would fall over the crowd as the announcer would declare the winning side for each event. When the winner was called, the flag holder would point to the team, and the captain of the event would run up, grab the flag, and run back to her teammates, who would be waiting to cheer and cry and hug each other.

Precise choreography and matching costumes created a uniformity that would reinforce the power of each routine. But even though there were hours and hours of planning, rehearsing, and performing to unify the group, I can't say there was unity. Cliques didn't fold. While new friendships were made, they were still defined by grade and social class. From the bleachers, each team may have looked like one, but there were still deep divides between individuals.

Uniformity is often misunderstood as unity. While uniformity may at times offer the appearance of unity—like my high-stepping marching team—unity does not mean the same thing. Uniformity is a state of homogeneity, where there is the appearance of sameness. This sameness might be physical (for instance, the costumes and steps in my marching team), or it might be mutual commitment to an ideal or philosophy. Uniformity runs the risk of banishing those who might not be in full agreement, or those who stray from the "norm" (which is why I was never selected for the modern dance team—my two left feet caused me to stray too far from the routine and the hope of a winning team). Unity, however, doesn't erase differences and disagreements. It requires a willingness to live with ambiguity as we come together for a greater purpose than our individual agendas. Without this space for difference, uniformity may result in greater disunity rather than unity.

## WHEN OPINIONS RULE

John Wesley, the founder of Methodism, understood the difference between uniformity and unity: "As to all opinions which do not strike at the root of Christianity, we think and let think."[1] In this way, Wesley crafted a way for the community to find their unity while at the same time allowing individual conscience and experience to flourish: "In essentials, unity; in non-essentials, liberty; and in all things, charity."[2]

The present crisis of possible division in The United Methodist Church has been caused by taking a nonessential—a position on homosexuality—and raising it to an essential on par with our understanding of the Trinity, the role of the sacraments, salvation through Jesus Christ, and so on. Instead of allowing liberty throughout our connection and acknowledging how God has moved in the lives of LGBTQ persons, the denomination has condemned homosexuality and expected uniformity on this issue, even when some local churches, boards of ordained ministries, annual conferences, and bishops have found this condemnation to be unwarranted. The United Methodist Church has sacrificed unity by enforcing uniformity on an issue that is nonessential to the faith we share.

This uniformity has been reinforced at every General Conference since 1972, when delegates voted to amend a Social Principle (see pp. 21–22) affirming the sacred worth of homosexual persons by adding the line: "though we do not condone the practice of homosexuality and consider this practice incompatible with Christian teaching."

This amendment was accepted, and a purely pastoral response to society's persecution of the LGBTQ community was turned into a statement of condemnation, impacting the conversation within the denomination regarding homosexuality ever since. It has been the foundation for denying LGBTQ persons the opportunity to be married by their pastors in the church they attend, for refusing to acknowledge the call of God in the lives of LGBTQ persons, forbidding LGBTQ persons from serving openly as pastors, and even creating a funding ban that denied the use of any general church money that could be construed as condoning homosexuality.

At every General Conference since 1972, matters related to homosexuality have dominated the agenda. While delegates have voted to retain the language and even tighten restrictions regarding LGBTQ people, the vote count reveals the denomination is not of one mind regarding homosexuality. However, the decision-making process of General Conference requires uniformity even when unity is lacking.

The use of parliamentary procedure as a way to make decisions for the denomination creates a false sense of unity. The purpose of Robert's Rules of Order, which provides the structure for parliamentary procedure, is to help a group make decisions in a way that is orderly and efficient.

Given that General Conference meets once every four years for less than two weeks at a time, bringing together up to 1,000 delegates from around the world to make decisions on approximately 1,000 proposals and petitions that will guide the church for the coming four years, having a process that uses delegates' time well is critical.

However, the problem with Robert's Rules of Order is that the majority makes the rules, creating winners (those in the majority) and losers (those in the minority). What happens when the church uses a decision-making process that creates winners and losers? Should there be winners and losers in the church? When something passes with only a 55 percent majority, there is little unity. Ask any local church leader if they would take a critical vote at their church knowing there was not a large majority of the church in favor of it, and they would probably respond no—to take a vote when the congregation is so divided further fractures unity.

This has been the case with the issue of homosexuality in The United Methodist Church. Even when the voting margin has been narrow, the majority prevents the body from acknowledging in its governing document the truth that is revealed by its voting patterns: the UMC is not of one mind regarding homosexuality. As a result, rules have tightened as the majority has tried to create unity through uniformity instead of recognizing that there is a wide range of understandings regarding homosexuality within the church.

## MAKING DECISIONS TOGETHER

I believe a healthier model for decision making within the church is found in consensus building. This allows the multiple truths that are held to come together for shared wisdom to shape and mold an outcome that all can live with. Consensus provides a way for all people to have a say in the decision but minimizes the creation of winners and losers as voters seek to support the best interests of the group.

I've been in groups that use the Five-Finger Voting model for creating consensus. This is a great way to receive recommendations and decide as a group whether to move forward with them or not. A proposal is made that addresses a problem. After fielding questions and providing responses, the group is invited to vote with their hands. Five fingers mean you are in total agreement and ready to provide active leadership to move forward with the proposal. Four fingers mean you strongly support the recommendation and will be active in its implementation, just not leading it. Three fingers mean you are good to go with the proposal. Two fingers mean you have reservations but will support the recommendation. One finger means you have strong reservations but will go along with the recommendation. A fist means you are blocking the recommendation because you feel it is harmful.

I discovered the power the consensus model can have in creating an agreement in community at Bethany UMC. It was the mid-1990s, and HIV/AIDS was still ravaging the gay community. Bethany had lost many beloved men to the disease. A major side effect to the disease and some of the drugs was known as "wasting syndrome"—drastic weight loss due to nausea and pain. One way to address this was medicinal marijuana, which had been proven to reduce the nausea and pain, enabling those with the disease to eat and gain vital nutrients, which in turn helped prolong their life.

Several medicinal marijuana clinics had opened up in San Francisco even though it was against the law. More and more HIV/AIDS patients began to receive prescriptions from their doctors to bring to the clinics to receive the marijuana. They found it indeed reduced pain and enabled them to eat. At one point, the attorney general of the state of California stepped in and ordered all the clinics closed. This created a medical crisis in the city. I received a call one day from the Rev. Jim Mitulski, pastor of the San Francisco Metropolitan Community Church (SF-MCC), asking if I, along with other progressive pastors, would consider allowing our churches to be used as a medicinal marijuana distribution site until the clinics could reopen.

Now this was never something I ever imagined I would be asked to do as part of my ministry. I still thought of myself as a rural church pastor in many ways. My learning curve in San Francisco was steep. But I had seen the impact of medicinal marijuana in the lives of some of my parishioners who were HIV-positive. So I agreed I would go to SF-MCC and observe what a pop-up clinic does. I went on a Friday and saw patients come in with prescriptions from their doctors. Volunteers would double-check the prescriptions, then hand over the medicinal marijuana to the patient.

I told those present that I would have to discuss this with my congregation and I would get back to them. I wasn't sure how I would discuss this with my parishioners. We had a good relationship and I didn't want to rock the boat. I had hoped to have a couple of days to think and pray about it. But I wasn't going to have the gift of time: the next morning I crawled out of bed, grabbed the newspaper, and got back in bed to read it. There was an article in the paper about San Francisco churches agreeing to become medicinal marijuana distribution sites, and my name was listed as one of the pastors who had agreed to it!

I broke out in a cold sweat, realizing that my parishioners were reading the same article. I began to think about how long it would take me to pack up and move, because surely they would feel betrayed by me and in this breach of trust, would no longer want me as their pastor. I approached Sunday morning with fear and dread.

When worship began, I took a few moments to address the congregation: "You probably read an article yesterday stating that I agreed that our church would become a medicinal marijuana distribution site. This was not accurate. I would never make such an impactful decision without engaging you. So I will send you everything I know about this request, including the legal ramifications. And I ask that you spend the next seven days praying about this: What would God have us do? We will then have an after-church forum next week to come to a decision."

The following Sunday church was packed—of course. Following worship, we stayed in the sanctuary and passed the microphone around so that people could say what was on their hearts. It was one of the most moving experiences I have ever had in a church.

"When my husband was dying of cancer, he was in terrible, terrible pain. I would have done anything to give him some relief. If I had known marijuana could have helped him, I would have gone anywhere to find it."

"What we're being asked to do is against the law . . . but then I ask myself, 'What would Jesus do?' Jesus broke laws if they prevented people from healing and wholeness. I think Jesus would want us to do this."

More and more people shared their thoughts and experiences, and it was clear we were arriving at consensus. Fears and concerns were voiced openly, and we grappled with those together. I marveled at the honesty and the ways the congregation engaged Scripture and spiritual resources to wrestle with what right action should be. We were about to conclude when one of the matriarchs, Inez McLaren, stood up.

"Wait one minute here," she began.

"Uh-oh," I thought, "Here it comes."

Inez continued, "Do you hear how we are talking about all this? We keep talking about 'them.' This isn't about 'them.' This is about us, about seeing people as our family. We can't just have people come in here, pick up what they need, and leave. We have to welcome them, we have to be here for them. They need to know they are not alone."

With that, consensus was achieved, and every time the clinic was hosted at Bethany, Inez and other Bethany members were present to provide warm and generous hospitality. To this day, many members point to this experience as a turning point in their discipleship and in the life of the congregation—there was a new depth of meaning as they followed God's call to provide hospitality, community, and care.

I think about this experience frequently. As a pastor, I learned so much. The first was that I hadn't given my congregation enough credit. They were more willing to step into the risks the gospel demands of us than I was. It has caused me to wonder: How often have I stopped a congregation's growth because I was afraid of the risks and challenges? If the power of the gospel has taken hold in the life of the congregation, why should I fear bringing controversial issues to them? Isn't God present in the controversies, expecting our engagement?

The other thing I learned was that consensus is a powerful way to make decisions. If we had simply voted—yes or no—to provide space for the clinic, there would have been hard, unresolved feelings that could have fractured the congregation. Instead, everyone brought their full self to the table, sharing honestly their fears, expectations, and understandings of where they felt God was leading us. It was through the shared wisdom that the Holy Spirit moved us, surprising us all as we said a communal yes. Deep unity was experienced that helped the congregation navigate other difficult decisions it faced.


**FROM RELIGIOUS RIGHT TO RIGHT RELATIONSHIP**

Unity is possible, even where there are deep theological divides. When the Religious Right ascended to power through the latter part of the twentieth century, it impacted San Francisco politics, particularly around civil rights for LGBTQ people. The Human Rights Commission of the city invited me to present a talk on the history of the Religious Right. I had already done some research on this topic for my Ph.D. dissertation. As a target of the Religious Right, I was curious about their theological orientation and commitment to social issues. In my dissertation, it was important to me as a scholar to not bring my own biases to the topic. I was excited to bring my research to the San Francisco government.

When I arrived at the chamber room in City Hall, I noted that in the gallery with observers was a pastor of a large San Francisco Baptist Church. His conservative stances were well-known, as he was a leader of the Religious Right within California.

The whole time I gave my speech, I was aware of his presence and the fact that, because he was sitting in the gallery and not in front of the committee members, he was unable to speak for himself and his colleagues about what they believed and why. At the conclusion of the meeting, he came up to me and said, "You did a good job explaining the topic, but you really don't know me." He was correct. I knew of the stances he had taken, the things he was for and against, but I didn't know him personally. "You are right," I said, "I don't know you. But I'd like to. Can we have lunch sometime?"

Once a week, throughout Lent of that year, I and another gay clergy had lunch with him. The conversation was at first cautious and tender as we learned of each other's call and the experiences we had had in ministry. Once we began to trust one another, the conversation grew bolder, as we asked one another hard questions about our respective controversial stances. We returned the boldness with honesty.

We learned that we were very different from each other. Yet, at the same time, we realized that there were places where we shared a common orientation: our love of God and God's people, our commitment to our call to ministry and a life of service, the claim Jesus had on our life, and our respect for Scripture. The mystery of the "other" gave way to newfound collegiality. I confess I looked forward to our lunches, and I suspect he did as well. He even told me that he was good friends with a nationally recognized conservative preacher: "I'd love for you to meet him," he said. "You'd really like him." Even though I had my deep reservations, I left the door open, saying, "That would be interesting."

From this common ground, we realized that there were things we could and should partner on, as a way to respond to human hurts and needs and provide a Christian witness to San Francisco. Literacy, homelessness, hunger, and other issues became places of collaboration and shared ministry.

These lunches made a profound impact on me. I recognized that unity was and is possible, even when we don't agree on all things. Requiring uniformity before we began our lunchtime meetings would have stunted our conversation and stifled the possibilities for shared ministry. This experience has helped me look for the common ground with those who, at first glance, seem to have little in common with me and in fact might even be unsupportive of who I am.

The great diversity of race, ethnicity, sexual orientation, gender identity, and lifestyle found in San Francisco is also reflected in its religious community. Through my involvement with the San Francisco Interfaith Council, I worked and worshiped beside Muslims, Sikhs, Buddhists, Jews, and every variation of Christianity possible. The organization had a major presence in the city and helped shape public opinion on several issues. Together, we also made a difference easing the suffering of our homeless brothers and sisters. In the winter months, churches, mosques, temples, and synagogues took turns hosting a winter homeless shelter. Each week, a different religious community would be the host. Other communities would provide the food and other assistance. It didn't just humanize and put a face on those who called our city streets their home. It also helped us learn from those whose religious practices were so unlike our own as we rubbed elbows preparing meals, serving our guests, and cleaning up.

Together, we were able to do far more than we could if we isolated ourselves and our ministries.

For me, these experiences put into practice Paul's understanding of Christian community:

> For just as the body is one and has many members, and all the members of the body, though many, are one body, so it is with Christ. For in the one Spirit we were all baptized into one body—Jews or Greeks, slaves or free—and we were all made to drink of one Spirit. Indeed, the body does not consist of one member but of many.
>
> (1 Cor. 12:12–14)

Requiring all to be an ear, or a foot, or an eye creates a dysfunction that limits the body—its ability to move, encounter, and shape the world. A well-functioning and healthy body is dependent on each part being recognized as vital to the well-being of the whole.

As a hiker, I need to care for my feet if I am going to traverse the wilderness. But other parts of my body are also important and necessary. Keeping my heart and lungs strong are critical if I am to climb up and down mountains. My eyes, ears, and nose help keep me on alert for danger. My arms and hands are needed to keep brush from my face (and also to pull myself up steep trails).

When did we decide some parts of the body of Christ were either less worthy of honor or even unwanted? What does it do to the wholeness and power we can achieve when we seek to exclude some from the body because "they aren't really like us"? We all possess unique gifts, given to us by God, necessary not only for our own well-being but for the well-being of our community.

Paul's words chide the arrogance of our exclusive practices:

> On the contrary, the members of the body that seem to be weaker are indispensable, and those members of the body that we think less honorable we clothe with greater honor, and our less respectable members are treated with greater respect; whereas our more respectable members do not need this. But God has so arranged the body, giving the greater honor to the inferior member, that there may be no dissension within the body, but the members may have the same care for one another. If one member suffers, all suffer together with it; if one member is honored, all rejoice together with it.
>
> (1 Cor. 12:22–26)

I reflect on verse 26 often: "If one member suffers, all suffer together with it." Do we even recognize the suffering we cause in our attempt at uniformity? Ask a child who is a little different, a college student who just doesn't quite fit in, someone with a disability, or someone who carries some minority status (whether race, class, sexual orientation, etc.) to the group they are in, and you will learn of how the inability to conform to the majority creates suffering. Difference threatens uniformity. The biggest injustice is asking someone to conform to a norm they are simply unable to meet because of their innate, unique personhood. This creates suffering and harm, the depth of which the majority are usually unaware.

This is the case around homosexuality and The United Methodist Church. Instead of the starting point

being the lives of LGBTQ people themselves, the church
has enforced a way of being that is harmful to its LGBTQ
members. Young people are not provided with healthy
LGBTQ role models. Lay leaders in a congregation are
forced to keep silent on a core part of who they are out of
fear of being shunned if they are honest and vulnerable with
those with whom they pray and work. People whose calls
have been affirmed are suddenly stripped of that affirmation once they come out.

Some within The United Methodist Church will
accept LGBTQ clergy providing they stay celibate. This
enforced celibacy continues harm by denying LGBTQ
people the possibility of deep, intimate, loving partnerships. The ability to have this kind of relationship was a
part of God's intention since the dawn of creation: "It's not
good that the human is alone" (Gen. 2:18, CEB).

By declaring LGBTQ relationships sinful, per-
verted, or evil, we are limiting love's power to flourish in
the world. This contradicts a basic understanding of love's
sacred nature given to us in Scripture:

> Beloved, let us love one another, because love is from
> God; everyone who loves is born of God and knows
> God. Whoever does not love does not know God,
> for God is love. God's love was revealed among us in
> this way: God sent his only Son into the world so that
> we might live through him. In this is love, not that we
> loved God but that he loved us and sent his Son to be
> the atoning sacrifice for our sins. Beloved, since God
> loved us so much, we also ought to love one another.
> No one has ever seen God; if we love one another,
> God lives in us, and his love is perfected in us.

By this we know that we abide in him and he in us, because he has given us of his Spirit. And we have seen and do testify that the Father has sent his Son as the Savior of the world. God abides in those who confess that Jesus is the Son of God, and they abide in God. So we have known and believe the love that God has for us.

God is love, and those who abide in love abide in God, and God abides in them. Love has been perfected among us in this: that we may have boldness on the day of judgment, because as he is, so are we in this world. There is no fear in love, but perfect love casts out fear; for fear has to do with punishment, and whoever fears has not reached perfection in love. We love because he first loved us. Those who say, "I love God," and hate their brothers or sisters, are liars; for those who do not love a brother or sister whom they have seen, cannot love God whom they have not seen. The commandment we have from him is this: those who love God must love their brothers and sisters also.

(1 John 4:7–21)

God is present in the lives and loves of LGBTQ people, even if the majority are unwilling or unable to admit this fact. God moves mysteriously and magnificently in our lives through love. Love helps us understand God's nature more fully. Why would we want to withhold that opportunity from anyone?

By refusing to bless LGBTQ relationships and requiring celibacy, we are hampering another's ability to be fully human. (Even Catholics, who require celibacy of their clergy, understand celibacy as a gift from God, not something one can impose on another.) Heterosexuality may be the majority expression of sexual orientation, but to require uniformity fails to take into account the fullness of diversity found in the human family.


## WE ARE ALL BLESSED WHEN LOVE CAN FLOURISH

Lolly and MaryAnn were nearly retired when I first met them shortly after I moved to San Francisco in 1989 to become a campus minister at San Francisco State University. They were members of the church I worshiped in and would later pastor, Bethany United Methodist Church. Lolly and MaryAnn met when they were in their twenties when they both worked for an airline. They fell in love and haven't been apart since then. Their love had to be navigated in the closet, however. This was 1960, before the Stonewall riots busted open closet doors across the United States. They lived through many changes, both within the LGBTQ community and within the larger culture. This was plainly evident at their thirtieth anniversary party, to which they invited me and several other younger LGBTQ members of Bethany.

They held their anniversary party in a side room of a well-known San Francisco restaurant. Around the walls of the room were collages made of pictures that chronicled the history of their relationship. Having worked for an airline meant that they were able to travel the globe together. There were photos from nearly every continent. It was a wonderful retrospective on their love.

As my contemporaries and I went from collage to collage, we noticed something in the early years of their relationship. Any formal picture or pictures taken outside their home included two men. We were confused by this

and asked Lolly and MaryAnn about it. They both chuck-
led at our naiveté. "Oh my," Lolly said, "back in the day we
couldn't let it be known that we were in a relationship—not
if we wanted to keep our jobs." MaryAnn picked up the
story: "We met these two guys and they became our best
friends. They, too, had met and fallen in love. We all knew
the risks of being gay at the time. Whenever there was an
event, we 'double-dated' so no one would be suspicious."

Lolly and MaryAnn are now nearing sixty years of
being together. They have seen so many changes regarding
LGBTQ rights. Could they, as they "double-dated" with a
gay couple, ever have imagined the possibility of legal marriage? The fact that their love has endured so many years
when so much was stacked against them reveals the truth
that love is of God, for God is love. How else could their
love have been sustained? As a result, they have blessed
so many of us through the generosity and compassion
that has been borne out of their relationship. To enforce a
heterosexual uniformity on Lolly and MaryAnn and other
LGBTQ couples would have meant that so many would
not have experienced the gifts that have come from two
people loving each other.

As Robin and I continued to provide annual leadership to the junior high church camp where we met, we
brought more and more volunteers from Bethany to be
camp counselors and cooks. Most of them were LGBTQ,
since that was the primary demographic of our younger
members.

We loved getting to know so many campers over their
three years of middle school. Some became counselors-in-
training and later counselors. Friendships were formed that
continue to this day. Our days were filled with Bible study,
hiking, swimming, games, and an evening program related

to the week's theme. Just prior to "lights out," the campers would gather at the campfire. New songs were learned
and beloved songs were sung. As the embers died down, a
camp staff member would provide a reflection of an important time in that person's life when God broke in.

Our counselors treated our campers with much
respect, being as honest as they could in ways that were
appropriate for the campers' ages. For many of our LGBTQ
staff, the coming out process was a deeply spiritual experience. As they claimed fully who they were, God was profoundly present. They shared with the campers the ways
they were bullied because they were different and how
much that filled them with despair and depression. Coming
out changed all that. It made them more sure of who they
were, of who God had created them to be. These campfire
talks were always moving and left many of our campers in
tears as they felt both the pain and joy of the person giving
the talk.

One of the staff that came from Bethany was Fritz.
Fritz had grown up in a United Methodist church in the
California Valley. He had been a leader in his youth group.
As he grew up and became aware of his sexual orientation, he suddenly had to deal with a church that would
reject him because he was gay. Instead of becoming bitter
or leaving the church, he dug in and became a leader as
an adult. He was an early member of Affirmation, a caucus within the denomination for LGBT concerns.[3] He was
also involved in the leadership at Bethany. Over the years I
served there, he was chair of the staff-parish relations committee, taught Sunday school, encouraged Bethany's social
witness in the city and in the world, and was a key member of the church's reconciling committee. Fritz had been
shaped by the conference's camping program as a youth

and loved returning to camp as the cook to give back a little of what had been given to him as a youngster.

The day after Fritz gave his campfire talk, which included his coming out story, I overheard several of our campers talking with each other.

"Can you believe Fritz is gay?" said Janet. "I had no idea!"

"Me neither," others chimed in.

Janet continued, "My mother said that gay people go against God's plan. She says they are evil and will go to hell when they die."

There was silence as they all pondered this for a few moments.

"But look at Fritz! He cooks us all such good food! Every year, he makes the menu better and better. I know he really cares about us. And I see the way he loves God . . ." There was the slightest of pauses as Janet came to a realization: "I think my mother is wrong."

It was Fritz's love of God and God's people that caused Janet to consider her mother's words in a new light. This love opened Janet's heart and mind. Through Fritz's commitment to young people and the great care he offered them, Janet not only experienced Fritz in a new way, but also felt the love of God more fully. If we had censored Fritz, informing him that a central part of his personhood was unwanted, that he couldn't talk about himself in full and authentic ways, the campers would have missed out on an encounter with God, expanding their own understanding of what an authentic life lived in service to God looked like.

A facade of uniformity would have inhibited the love that unites us, this love that is born of God and is God. Unity without love is impossible, for love is the force that guides the way we relate to each other and move in the world together. Love doesn't force a sameness but frees us all to live lives of authenticity. Love humanizes the "other" and turns them into kin. With this kind of new awareness of our connection, we seek the best for each other, upholding the dignity of those who may seem most unlike us, yet in whom we recognize our connection as members of the human family.

There have been times when I have been challenged to enlarge my world by supporting those who were not like me. It has been love's demands that awakened me to stand with those who were suffering and experiencing injustice. The lessons were not easy to learn, and the repercussions continue to this day. But they have helped me live with a greater understanding of the power of unity to change the world through love.

One such lesson started with a phone call from the Rev. Deborah Lee, a remarkable pastor and activist in the San Francisco Bay Area. Deborah and I had collaborated on several projects over the years. While my ministry at Glide Memorial kept me pretty busy, whenever Deborah called to ask for my help on something, I always tried to say yes. One day, I received a call from her about an action being organized by "Dreamers," young people who were eligible for the Obama administration's deferred action offered to undocumented youth who were brought to this country when they were young. These young people had been given a reprieve from the stress of living with the constant threat of deportation to a country many had no memory of. They were attending school, working, and often supporting members of their family. The problem was that while they had newfound status in the United States, their parents did not. It was not uncommon for children to return home from school to an empty apartment because Immigration and Customs Enforcement (ICE) officers had raided the home, rounded up those who were undocumented, and sent them to deportation centers.

Deborah introduced me to some of the Dreamers, and they shared with me some of their lives. I heard stories that made my heart break. Yet, I also heard stories of hope, as they shared with me their visions for their futures and all they were doing to turn these visions into reality. They told me they had learned that many of their parents who had been taken into ICE custody were going to be loaded on a bus and taken to the San Francisco Airport for immediate deportation. The young people asked me, and several other Bay Area religious leaders, to stand with them as they blocked the bus from going to the airport.

I only had to take one more look at the faces in my office to say yes. I wasn't totally sure what they were asking of me, but I had already fallen in love with these young people who had been through so much. On the appointed day, I went to the gathering place. The energy was electric as I watched these young people at work, preparing for the action. Several languages were spoken, many cultures were present, but there was a spirit at work that guided the group and brought unity as they planned together. This was strengthened as we prayed together before we left the building. Those of many faiths and no faith joined hands and become one as a blessing was offered by one of my colleagues.

We made our way to a small green space across the street from the ICE office. Partially hidden from the street by the trees and bushes, we waited for a signal from those who were trying to appear nonchalant as they stood a couple of buildings down from the ICE compound. They signaled to us as a large gate swung open and a bus slowly pulled out.

We immediately made our way across the street, blocking the bus once it had fully emerged from the gate. Dreamers stood at the front of the bus. Other Dreamers, along with my colleagues and I, stood at the rear. The bus could not move forward or back without running over the group. It was stuck.

We sat down and the chanting began. ICE officers began to surround us, but the young people stood their ground. I sat between two young men. We sat on the cold asphalt for hours. During that time, my love and admiration for them grew and grew. I was so moved by their courage and grateful for their care of me. Approaching an age closer to their grandparents than their parents, I was not used to sitting cross-legged on a cold surface. They kept checking in to see how I was doing and supported my back when they noticed me squirming.

My tears began to flow when they started chanting, "Our parents are on this bus." I couldn't imagine the lives they had lived, all that they had to endure, but knowing that it was quite possible that some of these young people would never see their parents again moved me deeply.

ICE officers gave way to the city police. I had participated in acts of civil disobedience that involved SFPD before, so I wasn't concerned. SFPD had covered more than its share of protests and demonstrations, and we all knew the drill that would occur—they would give us a time limit to the protest, and if we didn't move they would arrest us.

But this time, the San Francisco officers stepped aside and Homeland Security officers moved onto the scene. This brought the thing to a whole new level. The officers informed us that if we were arrested we would face a minimum of thirty days in a federal prison. This made me break out into a cold sweat. If I stayed where I was, I was going to learn that orange really is the new black.

I began to wonder if it was time to break ranks and move to the sidelines, where I could protest but avoid a jail cell. But then I looked around me. I looked at the young men and women who were willing to risk everything to break the deportation cycle—even risking their own deportation. I looked at the young men on either side of me. It was love that kept me rooted to my spot on the street, as we found unity even across the differences of life experiences, language, and culture. Their lives now mattered to me, and I was not going to move from where I was as long as they were there.

Love surprises us by revealing the ways unity can be achieved across so many lines of difference. Love can even cause us to act in solidarity with those we don't know, with those whom we may never meet.

The shooting of a Bible study group at Emanuel African Methodist Episcopal (AME) Church in Charleston, South Carolina, on June 17, 2015, was horrifying. Dylann Roof, a twenty-one-year-old white male, attended the Bible study that night. Before the end of the study, he pulled out a gun and shot and killed nine people and injured three others. The racial motivations were clear: Roof was a known white supremacist. Lovingly known as "Mother Emanuel," Emanuel AME served the African American community.

Immediately following the shooting, we invited the community to Glide one evening to engage in actions of solidarity and healing. Notes to the congregation were written. Videos of people's testimonies were captured. Signs proclaiming #WeAreAllMotherEmanuel were created to show our commitment to stand with those who were suffering and to seek to end racial violence. It was a powerful time in our community as the love we experienced at Glide was extended to those at Mother Emanuel.

Shortly after the shooting, there was a spike in acts of harassment and violence against mosques across the United States. This was further compounded by then presidential candidate Donald Trump's call for a ban on all Muslims entering the country. Another call for solidarity went out to stand with our Muslim brothers and sisters, this time with signs proclaiming #WeAreAllMuslim. It was a way to push back against Islamophobia and support Muslims across the United States.

I made my sign and had a staff member take a picture of me in one of my preaching robes, in front of one of Glide's stained glass windows. I then posted the picture on Instagram and Twitter. I was unprepared for the vile response to that picture. I was stunned by the amount of Islamophobia that was expressed. The hatred and venom was shocking.

Since July 2016, that picture has been circulated by those opposed to my election with no explanation of the background to it. A sign that was meant to express loving another so deeply that their pain became our own was misrepresented and used to further divide. I am fascinated by the fact that a picture seeking to reflect the love that Christ gave us has elicited so much hatred. God through Jesus Christ identified so closely with us that God became one with us. This wasn't what was expected of God. God was the Other, yet through Jesus, God comes near to us, becoming one of us with all the vulnerability that being human holds. This identification with us, this oneness, changed the divine-human relationship. We are called to offer that same solidarity to others as Christ has shown us.

This experience taught me so much. It opened my eyes to what Muslims experience every day and made me even more committed to standing with them in solidarity and support. Love requires nothing less from me.

When we choose to live our lives from a place of love, we find ourselves discovering the innate thread of connection that is found throughout creation. We move through the world knowing that each step, every action reverberates far beyond us and touches all living things. When our hearts are open to those whose lives look so different from ours, God keeps showing up in unlikely people and overlooked places. This becomes the seed that bears the fruit of unity.

Chapter 6

# WE EAT
# WITH PEOPLE WE LOVE

Ever since The United Methodist Church began to tighten ordination restrictions on LGBTQ people, friends and colleagues from more welcoming denominations have asked me, "Why do you stay in a denomination that is hostile to LGBTQ people?" Likewise, following my election to the episcopacy, more-conservative United Methodists don't ask but tell me, "You need to leave The United Methodist Church."

My friends in more welcoming denominations can't understand why I and countless others stay in a denomination that has stated, General Conference after General Conference, that LGBTQ people need not apply for ordination, that our commitment to love and honor our partners may not be recognized, and that even formally discussing our lives can threaten the financial health of General Church boards and agencies because a funding ban prohibits anything that smacks of "condoning" homosexuality. Why stay in a denomination that fails to recognize LGBTQ people as beloved children of God and members of the body of Christ?

These attitudes are present in the comments of those who not so kindly tell me to leave. For them, the rules of the church trump my own personal relationship with Jesus Christ, God's call to me, and the fact that I have faithfully served The United Methodist Church all my life. Some refuse to serve alongside me in church functions. Others send nasty notes.

I have always been taken aback by these questions, comments, and actions. Why do I stay? I stay because it is my spiritual home. It is where I have had a profound relationship with God, have had my living informed by Jesus Christ, and have found my path illumined by the Holy Spirit. It is the place where God's unfailing grace was not just talked about but experienced through the life of the community. The United Methodist Church has taught me to sing out my faith the way John Wesley expected: "Sing lustily and with a good courage."[1]

The United Methodist Church made a promise to me at my baptism. This promise was reaffirmed at my confirmation as a preteen and sealed at my ordination:

> Through baptism, God calls and commissions persons to the general ministry of all Christian believers (see 1992 Book of Discipline, ¶¶ 101–7). This ministry, in which we participate both individually and corporately, is the activity of discipleship. It is grounded upon the awareness that we have been called into a new relationship not only with God, but also with the world. The task of Christians is to embody the gospel and the church in the world. We exercise our calling as Christians by prayer, by witnessing to the good news of salvation in Christ, by caring for and serving other people, and by working toward reconciliation, justice, and peace, in the world. This is the universal priesthood of all believers.

From within this general ministry of all believers, God calls and the church authorizes some persons for the task of representative ministry (see 1992 Book of Discipline, ¶¶ 108–110).[2]

Baptism is a rite in which the entire community participates, as it receives a new member of the faith. "Baptism brings us into union with Christ, with each other, and with the Church in every time and place. Through this sign and seal of our common discipleship, our equality in Christ is made manifest (Galatians 3:27–28)."[3] As I grew more fully into the person God intended, the church broke its promise to me, of my unity with them as an equal in Christ, even though it continued to affirm the gifts and grace I possessed for ordained ministry. By declaring that homosexuality is "incompatible with Christian teaching," it made a pronouncement upon my life that separated me from the community of faith.

The United Methodist Church breaks its promise to every LGBTQ person who has found their heart "strangely warmed" by the grace of God through the ministries of its congregations. We who are LGBTQ are keenly aware of this broken promise, and it leaves us baffled by the boldness of the church to deny God's grace, which has moved in our lives. After all, it was the church that taught us to recognize and receive this grace in the first place!

The remarkable thing is that in spite of this unholy treatment, LGBTQ people continue to not only live lives of joy, but bring that joy into countless sanctuaries, seminaries, youth groups, and choirs. The spirituality found in Methodism has given us a spirit that cannot be diminished by the hostilities we have encountered.

## CLOSED DOORS, OPEN HEARTS

In 1996, I was chair of the Reconciling Ministries Network
(RMN) board of directors (at the time it was known as the
Reconciling Congregation Program), an unofficial United
Methodist connection of churches, campus ministries, and
groups that formally declared themselves to be in ministry
with and for all people, regardless of sexual orientation or
gender identity. The program started in 1984, when the
denomination began to restrict more fully the participation
of LGBTQ people in the life of the church. Shortly after
that year's General Conference, two churches—Washington
Square UMC in Manhattan and Wesley UMC in Fresno,
California—declared themselves to be reconciling churches.
With their declaration, a movement—headed at the time by
Beth Richardson and Mark Bowman—began. As of January
2018, RMN now includes 893 reconciling communities.[4]

With each successive General Conference including
more and more anti-LGBTQ policies, RMN decided to
mobilize members from across the country to be present at
the 1996 General Conference in Denver, Colorado. With
the creative leadership of the Rev. Bonnie Beckonchrist
from Northern Illinois and others, the "Open the Doors"
campaign was implemented. Signs of welcome and "open
the doors" were printed in several languages and placed in
restaurants surrounding the convention center where the
delegates would dine during meal breaks. Door mats with
sayings like "Jesus opened doors, and you can, too" were
placed in front of individual hotel room doors of delegates.
Knock, knock jokes were bantered about. Reconciling volunteers were present when delegates were arriving or leaving the convention center, literally opening the doors for
the delegates.

There were some delegates who refused to receive even these simple signs of gracious hospitality. Seeing an LGBTQ person or ally holding the door open for them, they quickly turned away to find a door no one was holding open. Others could not acknowledge those who were holding the doors open, not even looking them in the eyes or offering a "thank you."

There were signs of hope for those who were waiting for the church to "open the doors" and replace the condemning language with something more life-giving and representative of the wideness of God's grace and mercy. As General Conference began, fifteen active and retired bishops broke ranks with their colleagues and wrote a letter to the denomination, encouraging decisions that would help The United Methodist Church become more inclusive. Even then First Lady Hillary Clinton, a lifelong Methodist, encouraged the denomination to "open the doors" of the church in her address to General Conference.

When the plenary session turned to votes regarding homosexuality, reconciling volunteers sat in the bleachers watching the debates. We were noticeably younger than the delegates—many of us were in our twenties and thirties, and this was our first time at a General Conference. Surely the delegates had seen us, had experienced our love of God and the church, had experienced a change of heart that now moved them to desire a church with open doors? We all held our breath when the voting occurred. And we were all crushed when the church decided by a vote of 577-378 to retain the discriminatory language. We were also horrified as the church created even more anti-LGBTQ policies. Even though it passed a resolution calling for the US military not to ban people from serving in the military based on sexual orientation, the delegates added the phrase "self-avowed practicing homosexual" as a bar to ordination. Additionally, the delegates approved a position that homosexual unions shall not be conducted by United Methodist clergy nor be allowed to be celebrated in United Methodist churches.

Following these votes, we gathered in a large room together. Some were shell-shocked. How could the church do this to us? Don't they know we are their sons and daughters? Others wept openly. Deep sobs from broken hearts and wounded souls echoed across the room. But as Scripture reminds us, "Weeping may linger for the night, but joy comes with the morning" (Ps. 30:5b). Someone began to sing and one by one, others joined in. Hand reached for hand until we were all one body, singing and swaying. Prayer followed. We brought all our disappointment, pain, and feelings of rejection to God. God didn't leave us desolate but came into that room and rested on each one present, providing healing and restoring hope.

We discovered that there was a gay bar next to the convention center, and many of us moved from the convention center to the bar. The irony of that move didn't escape us. For generations, gay bars provided what the church couldn't or wouldn't—a place of sanctuary and safety where we could be fully ourselves without fear. We gathered the small tables together and talked of our hopes and dreams for the church's future. We still believed in the church even when it didn't believe in us. That bar became sacred space where we shared our faith journeys and coming out stories. We noted how entwined the two are. We spoke of our calls to ordained ministry and of the price we would have to pay in order to be faithful to that call—willingly hiding an essential part of who we were in order to serve. Not one person talked of leaving the church, but in fact there was a reaffirmation of our commitment to live out our callings in The United Methodist Church.

As we continued to converse, the somber tone turned. We reminded one another of the essential joy found in faith. We experienced the truth that resiliency is buoyed by joy. Laughter began to bubble up. Friendships were formed and deepened as a playful repartee was shared. We acknowledged that we were hopelessly in love with both God and the church. We were gay church geeks.

For each successive General Conference since then, the Reconciling Ministries Network has provided a witness at the meeting, bringing together LGBTQ people and allies in an attempt to share with delegates a glimpse of our lives. The petitions regarding homosexuality are not about an issue to be voted up or down. They are about *us*—our faith, our love, and our call. At each General Conference, new faces join seasoned members of the movement for full inclusion: young people fresh out of high school youth groups and now in college, parents whose children have come out in the four years since the last General Conference, pastors who know it is time to take a visible and vocal stance for a place at God's table for all God's children.

It's hard to watch these newcomers experience the deep pain of the church's refusal to acknowledge the reality that we are present in pews and pulpits across the United Methodist connection. They come with such hope. It was the church, after all, that gave them that hope. I watch them as the votes are cast, and my heart breaks with theirs as I see the disbelief and utter shock that the church can treat them/ us so callously. As one young person asked me through his tears, "Why do they hate us so?"

There were lots of college students, seminarians, and parents at the 2012 General Conference, working for full inclusion. This time, a broad alliance that shared a common orientation to justice was formed, called "Love Your Neighbor Coalition" (LYNC).[5] LYNC not only had a legislative agenda it was pursuing, but also sought to provide education and witness. Theologian James Cone lectured on black liberation theology. Daily worship grounded the volunteers. Young people engaged in street theater. A central part of LYNC's witness was the offer of hospitality to delegates with free meals served in the LYNC Tabernacle, a large tent across the street from the convention center.

As the petitions pertaining to matters of LGBTQ persons in the church were presented in the plenary session, LYNC volunteers moved down from the bleachers and stood at the rail surrounding the main floor of the conference, heads bowed in silent prayer. In spite of the efforts of the coalition, General Conference again voted to retain all anti-LGBTQ language and policies.

Feeling defeated once again, we retreated as General Conference concluded. But once again, we discovered a gay bar near the convention center. This time, we took to the dance floor, embodying the Psalmist who declared, "You have turned my mourning into dancing" (Ps. 30:11). The Spirit's joy cannot be dampened by hardened hearts. The love and joy we brought to the dance floor was contagious. As the bar closed and we spilled out into the steamy Tampa night, we didn't want to leave each other yet. We had been through so much together, and even though General Conference disappointed us one more time, the power of our love would not allow us to feel defeated.

So we did what Christians have done for centuries. We broke bread together. There was a taco shop next to the bar that was still open, and we spilled into it, arm in arm. Tacos were ordered and served up, and, just like the disciples' eyes that were opened as they feasted with a stranger from the Emmaus road, so were our own: Christ was with us. He had promised to be with us always, and that night we were reminded of that promise as we ate our tacos together.

Looking at the faces of those around me, I recognized what a resilient lot we were. If we could still hold this much joy in spite of the church's pronouncement on our lives, the church needed us more than it realized. That evening reminded me that Christ's body refuses to remain broken. Though human laws might seek to fracture the body, when attempts to leave some people outside the family of faith nearly amputates parts of the body, the power of the Holy Spirit does not allow us to remain in that broken, sad state. The Spirit blows in and unites us, sometimes in spite of ourselves.

## THE FAMILY TABLE

Probably the biggest lessons I learned about navigating life and deepening relationships were taught at mealtimes. The family dinner table of my childhood was a raucous place. It was at the table that we brought all the goings-on of our day and set them before each other. "I can't believe what happened in math class today!" " . . . and then Stevie dropped his books right on my foot." "Betty and I really got into it." It was the place to express not only what happened to us while we were apart from each other, but also the tensions we shared: "Ali, you took my favorite sweater without asking!" "Hey, I did the dishes last night." "Can't Lauren do something for once?"

Chores were complained about, renegotiated, and redistributed. Sometimes, silence settled in as one of us softly expressed a hurt we carried. Angry words were expressed but not held long. The one thing that was never tolerated was leaving the table without being excused. And one was never banished from the table because one's behavior was thought to be unacceptable. Staying at the table was the expectation, and my mother never made an exception for this rule.

This rule was reinforced with extended family, with whom we spent a lot of time. Whether with aunts and cousins who might come to visit us on Long Island, or with my mother's family in Nova Scotia or my father's family in Astoria, Queens, even as the dinner table stretched to include more people, opting out or leaving as the conversation turned controversial or heated was not allowed.

Grandma Oliveto's table literally groaned with the amount of food that was set on it. Grandma and Grandpa Oliveto were Italian immigrants. When we arrived at their third-floor walk-up, the apartment had the inviting aroma of garlic and simmering tomato sauce. The kitchen table was covered in thumb-imprinted gnocchi, which my grandmother had made and laid out to dry before they would be plopped into boiling water, to emerge plump and full. On top of the stove was a plate overflowing with freshly cooked meatballs, waiting to be submersed in the sauce. In the tiny living room, plates of antipasto dishes—olives, cheeses, pepperoni, peppers, and anchovies—covered every table.

Slowly the clan would arrive: my father's brothers and their families would converge from around the New York City metropolitan area. Sometimes, my grandparents' siblings and their families joined us as well. We kids would first run to the kitchen, which could barely hold us due to its size, and inspect Grandma's culinary works. We all stood by the stove, coveting the shiny meatballs, waiting for Grandma to offer us one to "try" before she placed them into the sauce.

We then all moved into the living room. The adults sat on the sofa and chairs while the rest of us went from table to table, snacking on the antipasto before running into my grandparents' bedroom to look out the window and spot the Empire State Building in the distance. Living out on Long Island, my sisters and I thought it was such an amazing sight to see from my grandparents' bedroom window.

Dinner moved into the dining room, which had been converted from a bedroom that my dad and his brothers once shared. No matter how many arrived in the apartment for dinner, there were always enough seats—as well as food—for everyone. Wine was poured and the eating—well, not so much commenced, since it started once we had entered the apartment—continued in earnest.

As in a typical Italian household, these family meals lasted hours. First, Grandma placed a roast, potatoes, and vegetables on the table. I remember my cousins and I looking wide-eyed at one another: Where was Grandma hiding all this food? After this course, what we kids were waiting for was *finally* before us—those thick, tasty gnocchi pillows and the preapproved meatballs, now sweetened by the tomato sauce. But this was not the end! Next came the salad. It was usually iceberg lettuce with lots of different vegetables. My grandmother's own signature dressing clung to the lettuce leaves, tangy and tart. The bowl was passed around, and salad took the place once filled by the gnocchi and meatballs.

There was a brief lull in the meal as plates were cleared. My grandmother made espresso, and Italian liqueurs as well as a variety of Italian desserts were set before us. Being loud at mealtime (as well as other times) seems to be a part of my family's DNA, and as each course was served and more wine poured, conversation grew more animated and increased a few decibels. Sibling rivalries reemerged, and political fault lines were intentionally stepped on. The banter bordered on contentious. We kids, stomachs feeling totally stuffed, could barely slither out of our seats to lie down under the table as the adults lit up their after-dinner cigars, filling the air with pungent smoke. At our parents' feet, we would doze in and out of consciousness, aware of the animated conversations occurring above us, feeling a well of love that seemed infinite. No amount of arguing could threaten this love, for we knew that by the time the dessert dishes were finally cleared and the bottles of liqueurs put away, hugs and kisses would be shared as we all went back to our respective homes.

This was the power that sharing a meal had over all who ate together. By the time I was old enough to prepare for confirmation, translating what I had experienced at my family's various dinner tables helped me understand what happened whenever the church had Communion: *we eat with people we love.*

I can clearly remember my confirmation. It was a beautiful May day on Long Island's South Shore. My church friends and I had had not just a year of confirmation classes together; we had grown up with each other through the ministries of the church: Sunday school classes, choirs, vacation Bible school. We all had received a Bible from the church when we were in the fourth grade. We had sung in numerous Christmas candlelight services, sitting in the choir loft, watching the light pass from candle to candle until the entire church was bathed in a beautiful light as we sang "Silent Night" acapella in four-part harmony.

For confirmation, we had all been given a white robe to wear. We were also given the gift of a Methodist hymnal—this was before the creation of The United Methodist Church—a sign of the high value our church put on its music ministry. Those of us who grew up in that church knew most of the hymns in that book by heart, thanks to Ken White and Julie Carney, our excellent music ministers. (This is no exaggeration. One year, Cathy Centabar, a youth group friend who also attended Drew University, and I were returning to Babylon during one of our breaks. The car's radio was broken, so we passed the time by starting with the first hymn in the hymnal, "O For a Thousand Tongues to Sing," and singing each hymn, page after page, even though we didn't have a hymnal with us. These hymns had become a part of us.)

During the confirmation ritual, we all said our vows, reaffirming promises that were made on our behalf at baptism. I remember thinking at the time, "This is the most important promise I am making in my life" (I had no idea there would be other promises). Then we were invited to kneel at the altar rail and receive Communion for the first time.

I knelt not only with the other confirmands but was also joined by my family. How right that felt. It was as if my heart had leapt out of my chest and surrounded us—my friends, my mom, my Aunt Connie, and my cousin Linda. At the same time, in this holy mystery we call Communion, I was aware of the presence of more than those who knelt with me. My arms, resting on the altar rail, felt the indentions of countless other arms and elbows of parishioners who had knelt in this very same place since the church was built in 1859. As I took the small, cubed piece of white bread and the small cup of grape juice, I was aware that I was taking part in a rite that extended two millennia. How many other hands had reached for the bread? How many others had raised the cup to their lips and tasted the sweetness of its contents? I knew that this meal connected me to Christ and, therefore, to all those who had ever taken part in this ritual.

Ever since then, Communion has played an important part of my spiritual life. Significant moments of my life have included this sacred meal—including my wedding. Marriage was not something LGBTQ people of my generation ever thought we'd do. When you come out, there are no road maps for how to live your life: no social blueprint for dating, partnering, and creating a life with someone else. There is a well-worn joke about this: What do lesbians bring on the second date? The U-Haul. This is because without the cultural steps to deepening relationship and commitment, the stereotype is that lesbians get involved too deeply, too quickly. Straight friends learn that one goes from flirting to dating to serious dating to engagement to marriage. LGBTQ people, until recently, weren't given these official steps and stages, nor were our relationships given legal protection or a sacred blessing from the church.

In 2004, when Mayor Gavin Newsom allowed the city and county of San Francisco's clerk office to issue marriage licenses to gay and lesbian people, it was as if all heaven had broken loose in the city. Love was literally busting out all over. Couples came from across the country to be married in that short window of opportunity. The line into the clerk's office wound its way through city hall, down the steps and around the block.

Robin and I had been dating for five years at this point. We had committed ourselves to one another, although not in a formal way. It was enticing to actually be able to marry, particularly since we had experienced a scare with Robin's health and realized there were no legal protections for the life we had begun to build together. But I didn't want to "elope." Having never thought marriage would ever be an option in my life, I realized that I wanted more than a quick city hall marriage. I wanted my family and dear friends present.

It was painful to watch the window close, as the courts put a stop to the weddings. We weren't sure if that opportunity would ever present itself again. When the Supreme Court struck down the Defense of Marriage Act in 2013, we decided it was time to plan our wedding. We knew we couldn't afford a San Francisco wedding. We also knew we didn't want a big wedding. We decided to have a small legal ceremony in San Francisco, followed by a four-day destination wedding in Mexico with our loved ones. One hundred family members and friends came from as far away as Nova Scotia to join us. It was by far the happiest weekend we have experienced together, as we watched people we loved from various stages and places in our lives get to know one another.

We had planned a couple of group activities during the weekend. One of them was an early morning Communion service on the beach. We asked three friends—the Rev. Tom Carney and the Rev. Liz Braddon, long-time friends from my home church, and the Rev. Theon Johnson III, the associate at Glide, to preside over Communion. We didn't think many people would come to this early morning event, but we knew we wanted to ground our wedding day with Communion. We were surprised as nearly all our guests joined us on the beach.

Each of our pastor friends shared a word about Communion. Tom talked of the importance of companionship

that is grounded in God and community, and spoke to us
of Ecclesiastes 4:9–12:

> Two are better than one, because they have a good
> reward for their toil. For if they fall, one will lift up the
> other; but woe to one who is alone and falls and does
> not have another to help. Again, if two lie together,
> they keep warm; but how can one keep warm alone?
> And though one might prevail against another, two
> will withstand one. A threefold cord is not quickly
> broken.

He then had each person or family group come to us,
join hands with us, and recite the Scripture to us. It was a
powerful reminder that love needs community to grow and
flourish. After this ritual, the bread and cup were raised,
reminding us of God's love that meets us in this meal. As
we shared the Communion elements, I was filled with deep
love, not only for those who were present for this special
day, but also for all those who couldn't be with us—their
faces were before me, and I felt within me rising up a love
and peace that passes all understanding.

This is the power of that meal. It creates community
that transcends not only our differences, but also time and
space. As we partake of the bread and cup, we are reminded
that we are called to a life of connection through the grace of
God. This knowledge compels a response from us, a way of
living that recognizes love's demands.

Once we feast on Christ, we live Christ. This was
modeled so powerfully for me when I was a small child.
My mother, by then a single parent, was juggling work and
three children under the age of ten. My sister Alison was a
toddler. Lauren, the youngest, was still in a high chair as

we finished up dinner one evening. My mother was cleaning off the table, and Ali was standing by the stairs going down into the basement. I saw Ali begin to lose her balance. Everything seemed to move in slow motion as she began to fall down the stairs toward the hard basement floor. Everything, that is, except my mother, who flew across the room and threw herself down the stairs so that Alison would fall on her, cushioning her fall. I watched as my mother's body thudded against the basement floor, and then heard an "uff" as Alison fell into her waiting arms. I then watched at the top of the stairs, as my mother clung to her middle child and wept. It is one of the few times I have ever seen my mother cry.

This self-sacrificial act, occurring after we had eaten dinner together, has left a profound mark on my life, teaching me about the depth of love we are to have for each other. It is one more thing that has helped me understand the power of the Communion meal. If we feast at Christ's table and don't live our lives seeking to care for others, putting the needs of others before our own comfort, have we really allowed the meal to fill us with the presence of Christ and the love of God that companions us in this meal?

As I ponder the brokenness in our world and the great polarities that are being created between people and between communities, I keep coming back to the power of meals, and specifically, for those of us who are Christian, the power of Communion. During a time when we have seemingly lost the capacity to feel for those who are different from us, to understand how our actions (and inactions) impact others in the world, and to honor the diversity that is inherent in the human family, I believe we need to come to Christ's table as often as possible.

## IN THE BREAKING OF BREAD

I love the story of the disciples on the road to Emmaus. In Luke's Gospel, this passage occurs after the women have gone to Jesus' tomb to tend to his body. They were stunned to find his body missing, and even more surprised to find two angelic visitors, who asked them, "Why do you look for the living among the dead? He is not here, but has risen" (Luke 24:5). The women ran to the disciples to tell them what they had seen and heard, but the eleven men dismissed the women's testimony.

Later that day, two of the disciples were walking on the Emmaus road. I often think about what it must've been like to be them: they had dropped everything to follow their teacher. They had believed with every cell in their body that Jesus was the one for whom they had been waiting. They had weathered the ups and downs of this new religious movement, with Jesus guiding them all the way. But they had been unprepared for the brutality and violence Jesus experienced, which left him hanging on a cross. How could this have happened? What was left for them? Could they just go back to their old lives, as if the few years they shared together had never happened?

They walked with heavy hearts and downcast spirits, still trying to process all that had happened. Then, someone caught up with them and began to walk alongside them— they didn't recognize the man as someone they knew. He asked about their conversation, and they must've thought he was crazy—hadn't he heard about what had occurred over the last three days? They began to tell him of it all, in particular the fact that Jesus' tomb was empty.

The stranger began to review Scripture with them, discussing all the things that had been said about the

Messiah. There must've been something to his presence, because when it looked like he was going to leave them, they asked him to say and join them for a meal. It was as the stranger took the bread, blessed it, and broke it that their eyes were opened and they realized that this was their teacher! The whole time they had been walking with Jesus.

Once they finally recognized him, he vanished from their sight. They began to share what they felt as he walked with them, how something stirred in them, even though they didn't know what it was. They ran to tell the others "how he had been made known to them in the breaking of the bread" (Luke 24:35).

I love this narrative because it reminds us of what happens when we eat together—Christ is with us. Our eyes and hearts are opened to those in our midst whom we may have overlooked and don't even see. It is in this opening that we are connected to others in deeply powerful ways. We once were blind to each other, but now we see. In our seeing, how we relate to one another changes.

My own eyes have been opened time and time again when I have stayed at the table with those I have discounted or simply chosen to not engage. Following the 2012 General Conference, there was a movement within my annual conference, California-Nevada, to research ways we could stay in The United Methodist Church and still be fully welcoming of LGBTQ people. A petition was brought before the body to create a task force to do this work. Before it was passed it was amended. Instead of a solely progressive team, the amendment called for the task force to include the full theological spectrum found in the conference. This did not settle well with progressives, myself included. How could we create a plan for inclusivity with those who were not supportive of a fully inclusive church? Our own commitment to inclusion ended where their theological commitments began.

I was chosen to be on the task force, but I wasn't happy about it. I looked at the roster and felt hopeless seeing the other names on the list. I went to the meetings with much resentment. When I looked around the room and saw my conservative colleagues, I just wanted to give up even trying to do the work we had been given. I didn't see my conservative colleagues as people, but as obstacles and issues. I was doing to them exactly what I accused them of doing to me. This realization didn't come quickly or easily to me, I confess. It happened over time. Meeting after meeting, we sat together and shared meals together. Then, something shifted. Instead of focusing on the task, we began to focus on each other. We spoke with one another about our call stories. We expressed our love for God. We told one another of our ministry experiences and how this work moved us deeply. We talked about our great love of the church.

As we found that common ground, we began to go deeper in our sharing, discussing how we first learned about sex, how we came to an understanding of our own sexuality, and what the church taught us about our bodies and our sexualities. We trusted each other enough to share some secrets we had never uttered aloud, ways we had been mistreated by others that impacted our self-understanding. The conversation was life-giving and healing.

All this happened as we filled one another's cups with coffee or passed around cans of soda. It happened as we cut up sandwiches for one another. We stopped seeing each other as adversaries as we felt the presence of Christ in the breaking of bread. And all of us were changed.

We concluded our task force work in a way that no one in the conference expected, and it made neither conference progressives nor conservatives very happy, at least at first. Instead of a clear path forward that would free us from each other, we had discovered that we needed each other if our ministries were to express the fullness of God's love and reach the great diversity of God's people.

We decided that merely writing a paragraph or two on the process we had engaged in wasn't enough. I wrote a script, and the Rev. Stephen Pudinski (one of the more conservative members of the committee) and I presented it before the clergy and laity gathered for Annual Conference in June of 2014. People knew who we were. They knew we were from opposite "camps" in the church. We stood on opposite ends of the dais, and what we said surprised them all:

> STEVE: Last fall we were invited to be on the Study Committee for an Inclusive Conference.
> KAREN: And when we arrived at the meeting we discovered—
> TOGETHER: He/She was there!
> KAREN: Really? Was I going to get what I hoped for with him there?
> STEVE: Really? It feels like a waste of my time if I have to work with her.
> KAREN: We are so different.
> STEVE: Good News.
> KAREN: Reconciling.
> STEVE: Evangelical.
> KAREN: Progressive.
> STEVE: Male.
> KAREN: Female.
> STEVE: Straight.
> KAREN: Queer.
> TOGETHER: Could anything good come from this?

STEVE: Then it stopped being about us.

KAREN: And began being about the Holy Spirit.

*(Start slowly moving toward each other.)*

STEVE: We talked about our love of God . . .

KAREN: . . . our love of Jesus . . .

STEVE: . . . our love of The United Methodist Church . . .

KAREN: . . . our love of the people of God . . .

STEVE: . . . our love of ministry . . .

KAREN: . . . our love of our Wesleyan heritage and spirituality.

TOGETHER: We realized we weren't that different.

STEVE: We both wanted the same thing.

KAREN: A vibrant church . . .

STEVE: . . . a Beloved Community . . .

KAREN: . . . and a way to move beyond the current polarization of our denomination.

STEVE: As we listened to each other . . .

TOGETHER: We grew to respect and even love one another.

*(Pause, as if surprised!)*

KAREN: The United Methodist Church needs Steve.

STEVE: The United Methodist Church needs Karen.

KAREN: Steve can extend the love of God to people I can't.

STEVE: Karen can extend the love of God to people I can't.

KAREN: I need Steve as a colleague.

STEVE: I need Karen as a colleague.

TOGETHER: We need each other if we are to be church together.

STEVE: We need to move past lines in a Discipline that divide rather than unite us.

KAREN: We need to admit the truth in Cal-Nevada, what the General Church is unable to acknowledge:

TOGETHER: We are not of one mind regarding homosexuality.

STEVE: But faithful ministry is happening across the theological spectrum.

KAREN: And the fruits of the Spirit are being expressed in diverse lives.

STEVE: We are learning to live into our differences.

KAREN: We are learning a more honest way of being in community.

TOGETHER: And it is changing me.

STEVE: We invite you to experience the power of holy conferencing.

KAREN: To join with people in our annual conference in the coming months.

TOGETHER: And allow the Holy Spirit to lead us all to a place we hadn't intended to go. Together.

Every word was true for both of us. And it resonated with those who listened to us,[6] By staying at the table together, we offered hope for a church that was terribly divided. In the coming months, the process our task force had used was replicated throughout the annual conference. Friendships formed where there once was mistrust. New partnerships in ministry were made possible because we stopped "othering" and instead saw each other,

perhaps for the first time, as members together in the body
of Christ.

It all happened because we were willing to stay at the
table together. We all could have stayed in our cultural and
theological corners and refused to engage with each other.
By staying at the table, the myths we had about each other
were stripped away and we were left with the truth found in
one another's lives. This opened our hearts to one another
and forged friendships and even love where there was once
distrust and animosity. What is it about a meal that helps us
be vulnerable with each other?

## COMING TOGETHER AT CHRIST'S TABLE

Within every religious tradition, the eating of a meal is
spiritually significant. It is through a ritual meal that new
kinship lines are drawn. Instead of defining family by one's
lineage, it is remade through the mystery of ritual. This is
how the body of Christ, for instance, is reconstituted every
time we partake in the Communion meal. Like those disciples in mourning, our eyes, too, are opened to realize God
is with us and working through all of us, including those we
once dismissed and discounted.

This is how community starts. This is the way that
paves the way for healing. This is what is necessary in a
world that no longer knows how to hold the tension of
differences.

There was one General Conference that hit home
the power of Christ's Table to tear down the walls and create connection with those who are unlike us. My heart has
been forever changed by the experience. It was during a
time when the Institute on Religion and Democracy[7] (IRD)

had written inflammatory things about me and was seeking to mobilize people against me and my ministry. They did this without knowing me personally or interviewing me for their articles and blogs. Because of this treatment, I found myself "othering" the staff of the IRD. I didn't want to see any of them—I didn't even want to be in the same room as one of them. I had made them my enemy.

The Reconciling Ministries Network was hosting a worship service at the midpoint of the ten-day General Conference meeting, and I was asked to help serve Communion. After nearly a week of debates and rhetoric around LGBTQ issues, it was so wonderful to be around folks who were like me. My shoulders relaxed and my soul breathed again.

I was serving the bread, and as each person stood before me I'd look quickly at their name tag and then look them in the eye and say their name before offering them the bread with the words, "This is the body of Christ, offered to you." With that naming and with those words, I placed bread in their outstretched hands.

Then, I did a double take at the name tag of the person who was waiting to be served. "Mark, this is the body of Christ . . ." Mark. As in Mark Tooley. As in the current executive director of the IRD. So many feelings ran through my mind, body, and soul as I held the bread in my hands.

Here is the thing: that meal totally transformed my feelings toward Mark. Because, as a Christian, I believe certain things about Communion. "Since there is one loaf of bread, we who are many, are one body, because we all share the one loaf of bread" (1 Cor. 10:17, CEB). Communion creates new kinship lines. People we barely know, people we have never met, become our kin. With the offering of Christ's body, Mark stopped being my enemy and became my brother. And that has forever changed how I feel about him.

There is a song that is often song at inclusive church
meetings that keeps reminding me of God's wide invitation
to come to table together:

Come to the table of love!
Come to the table of love!
This is God's table, it's not yours or mine.
Come to the table of love!*

This table is not Mark's table, nor is it mine. It is
God's Table in which Christ's presence is felt and family
members we never met before are discovered. As I learned
over loud family suppers, we don't have to agree about
everything. Conversations can get heated, feelings might
get hurt, and buttons will most likely be pushed, but the
love remains, binding us even more tightly together as we
break bread with one another.

As we grow in our spirituality, we need to find
ways to make room at the Table for more. We need to
do the hard, internal work to discover our own blind-
ers, prejudices, and ways we foster othering in our lives
in order to celebrate diversity as a sign of God's infinite
imagination. We must practice a spirituality that deep-
ens our empathy with those around us. Henri Nouwen
reminds us that this

> grows with the inner recognition that your neighbor
> shares your humanity with you. This partnership cuts
> through all walls which might have kept you separate.
> Across all barriers of land and language, wealth and
> poverty, knowledge and ignorance, we are one, created

---

*"Come to the Table of Grace," by Barbara Hamm, © 2008 Hope Publishing Com-
pany, Carol Stream, IL 60188. All rights reserved. Used by permission.

from the same dust, subject to the same laws, destined for the same end. With this compassion you can say, "In the face of the oppressed I recognize my own face and in the hands of the oppressor I recognize my own hands. Their flesh is my flesh, their blood is my blood, their pain is my pain, their smile is my smile. . . . There is nothing in me that does not belong to them, too."[8]

We need to be vigilant in our words and actions, always asking ourselves: Is what I am saying, is what I am doing, increasing compassion and connection in the world, or rupturing relationship with others, with the divine, with the earth, with myself? These are difficult days. Our churches often resemble battlegrounds. The public square of our common life has lost much civility. We keep seeking to build walls of mistrust and misunderstanding rather than bridges of mutual commitment and compassion.

We need to reclaim our spiritual traditions more than ever before. We need to join together hearts and souls and hands for the hard work of protecting each one's dignity. May love be the guiding force in our relationships, in our churches, in our halls of government. May love propel us to move from segregated tables to those that bring us face-to-face with one another, so that the face of God becomes more visible. May love give us the capacity to extend community beyond the borders we currently have in place, so we can join hands with our brothers, our sisters, our siblings.

At the Table, enemies become friends, strangers become companions, and community is established and affirmed. Differences are not diminished but are welcomed. Across lines of difference, healthy community is formed through the sharing of life together. Our ability to have empathy strengthens our ability to love those who are not like us, even when we disagree.

May we learn to stay at the Table. Together.

# NOTES

## Introduction

1. Isaac Watts, "I Sing the Mighty Power of God," *Divine and Moral Songs for Children*, 1715.

2. John Wesley, Journal, March 4, 1738.

3. Michael Collins, *Carrying the Fire: An Astronaut's Journeys* (New York: Farrar, Straus, and Giroux, 1974).

4. Sultan bin Salman Al-Saud, Opening remarks offered at the First Congress of the Association of Space Explorers, Cernay, France, October 2, 1985.

5. Frank Borman, quoted in *Newsweek*, December 23, 1968.

## Chapter 1: The Fractured Family Table

1. Heather Mason Kiefer, "Empty Seats: Fewer Families Eat Together," *Gallup News*, January 20, 2004, http://www.gallup .com/poll/10336/Empty-Seats-Fewer-Families-Eat-Together .aspx.

2. Ibid.

3. Roberto A. Ferdman, "The Most American Thing There Is: Eating Alone," *Washington Post*, August 18, 2015, https://www .washingtonpost.com/news/wonk/wp/2015/08/18/eating-alone -is-a-fact-of-modern-american-life/?utm_term=.7a3dac4dbcc4.

4. In my own episcopal area, which includes Montana, Utah, Wyoming, Colorado, and a small section of Idaho, white supremacists have become emboldened by recent political events

and are more outspoken in their hate speech. For example, see Keila Szpaller and Gwen Florio, "White Supremacist Website Calls for Action in Montana," *The Missoulian,* December 19, 2016, http://missoulian.com/news/state-and-regional/white-supremacist-website-calls-for-action-in-montana/article_3b95f7d3-d6f5-5d2d-831c-d2c2cb647010.html.

5. "Post-Trump Victory Bullying, Harassment Reported in Schools," CBS News, November 13, 2016, http://www.cbsnews.com/news/post-trump-victory-bullying-harassment-reported-schools/.

6. "2016 Cyberbullying Data," Cyberbullying Research Center, November 26, 2016, https://cyberbullying.org/2016-cyberbullying-data.

7. John Wesley, *Thoughts upon Slavery* (Philadelphia: Joseph Crukshank, 1774), 56.

8. C. H. Phillips, *This History of the Colored Methodist Episcopal Church in America: Comprising Its Organization, Subsequent Development, and Present Status, Book One* (Jackson, TN: Publishing House of C.M.E. Church, 1925), 23.

9. Quoted in Pamela Crosby, "African Americans Gather to Remember Central Jurisdiction," UMNS, September 1, 2004, http://www.umc.org/news-and-media/african-americans-gather-to-remember-central-jurisdiction?_ga=2.158085242.1311678974.1499776242-1696528858.1499776242.

10. See Shaw's autobiography, *The Story of a Pioneer* (New York: Harper & Brothers, 1915) for more details of her life. It is available at http://www.gutenberg.org/files/354/354-h/354-h.htm.

11. General Conference is the top legislative body of The United Methodist Church. It occurs every four years, bringing together nearly one thousand delegates (half clergy and half laity) from across the global denomination. The General Conference determines all church matters, including budget, structure, and social witness for the denomination.

12. This phrase is from a poem by Lord Alfred Douglas, "Two Loves," and is often used as a veiled reference to homosexuality.

13. See www.rmnetwork.org for more information.

14. In The United Methodist Church, clergy are appointed to congregations by the bishop of their conference (regional area). District superintendents oversee smaller areas within each conference as directed by the bishop.

15. The United Methodist Church is made up of five US geographic jurisdictions that include the annual conferences within the area, as well as Central Conferences, which are groupings of annual conferences in Africa, Europe, and the Philippines. Each jurisdiction and Central Conference elects bishops to serve within their region.

16. Zygmunt Bauman, *Modernity and Ambivalence* (Oxford: Polity, 1991), 14.

## Chapter 2: Exercising Empathy

1. Paul S. Bellet, Michael J. Maloney, "The Importance of Empathy as an Interviewing Skill in Medicine," *JAMA* 226, no. 13 (October 2, 1991): 1831–32, doi:10.1001/jama.1991 .03470130111039.

2. Arlie Russell Hochschild, *Strangers in Their Own Land: Anger and Mourning on the American Right* (New York: New Press, 2016), 5.

3. "What Drives Trump Supporters? Sociologist Arlie Russell Hochschild on Anger and Mourning of the Right," interview, Democracy Now! (September 28, 2016), https://www .democracynow.org/2016/9/28/what_drives_trump_supporters _sociologist_arlie.

4. Nelle Morton, *The Journey Is Home* (Boston: Beacon Press, 1985), 55.

5. Daniel Burke, Religion News Service, "Methodists Maintain Homosexual Acts Are 'Incompatible with Christian

Teaching' at General Conference," *Huffington Post*, May 4, 2012, http://www.huffingtonpost.com/2012/05/04/methodists -homosexual-act-incompatible_n_1476042.html.

6. "Proceedings of the 2012 General Conference of The United Methodist Church," May 3, 2012, http://s3.amazonaws .com/Website_Properties/files_import/UMC_Files /GC2012%20DCA%20reports/5-5_DCA-VOL%2011 -PROCEEDINGS.PDF, 2711.

7. "Risk Factors for LGBTQ Youth," newsletter, The Institute for Innovation & Implementation, University of Maryland School of Social Work, n.d., https://theinstitute.umaryland .edu/newsletter/articles/June%20Newsletter_LGBTQLGBTQ _Risk_Factors.pdf.

8. Harper Lee, *To Kill a Mockingbird* (New York: Harper-Perennial Modern Classics, 2002), 33.

## Chapter 3: Leaning into Ambiguity

1. The Pew Global Attitudes Project, "World Publics Welcome Global Trade—But Not Immigration," October 4, 2007, www.pewglobal.org/files/pdf/258.pdf, 35.

2. James Fowler, *Stages of Faith: The Psychology of Human Development and the Quest for Meaning* (New York: Harper-Collins, 1995).

3. Quoted in Martin B. Copenhaver, "Jesus Is the Question," devotional, United Church of Christ, July 23, 2011, http://www .ucc.org/feed-your-spirit_daily-devotional_jesus-is-the-question.

4. Robert J. Dufford, "Be Not Afraid," © 1975, 1978, Robert J. Dufford and OCP Publications.

5. Anne Lamott, *Plan B: Further Thoughts on Faith* (New York: Riverhead Books, 2005), 256–57.

## Chapter 4: Diversity Is a Sign of Divinity

1. "Two-spirited" is a term used to describe individuals whose gender identity is both male and female.

2. Linda Emma, "Advantages and Disadvantages of Diversity in the Workplace," Small Business (undated article), *Houston Chronicle*, http://smallbusiness.chron.com/advantages-disadvantages-diversity-workplace-3041.html.

3. Matthew Yglesias, "Diverse Groups Make Better Decisions," *Slate*, January 21, 2014, http://www.slate.com/blogs/moneybox/2014/01/21/diverse_groups_make_better_decisions.html.

4. Kim Abreu, "The Myriad Benefits of Diversity in the Workplace," *Entrepreneur*, December 9, 2014, https://www.entrepreneur.com/article/240550.

5. Quoted in Ekatrina Walker, "Reaping the Benefits of Diversity for Modern Business Innovation," *Forbes*, January 14, 2014, https://www.forbes.com/sites/ekaterinawalter/2014/01/14/reaping-the-benefits-of-diversity-for-modern-business-innovation/#705983cf2a8f.

6. "Population Distribution by Race/Ethnicity," Kaiser Family Foundation, https://www.kff.org/other/state-indicator/distribution-by-raceethnicity/?currentTimeframe=0&selectedDistributions=white&sortModel=%7B%22colId%22:%22Location%22,%22sort%22:%22asc%22%7D.

7. Binny Trang, "Diverse Teams—Is This Good or Bad? And How to Manage a Diverse Team More Efficient [sic]?" March 30, 2015, https://binnytrang.wordpress.com/2015/03/30/145/.

8. Katherine Phillips, "How Diversity Makes Us Smarter," *Scientific American*, October 1, 2014, https://www.scientificamerican.com/article/how-diversity-makes-us-smarter.

9. Robin Showers, "Four Business Benefits of Diversity in the Workplace," blog, Brazen Technologies Inc., https://www.brazen.com/blog/recruiting-hr/benefits-of-diversity-in-the-workplace.

10. Benjamin Forman and Caroline Koch, "Geographic Segregation: The Role of Income Inequality," *Communities & Banking*, Federal Reserve Bank of Boston, August 6, 2012, https://www.bostonfed.org/publications/communities-and-banking/2012/fall/geographic-segregation-the-role-of-income-inequality.aspx.

11. Alvin Chang, "White America Is Slowly Self-Segregating," *Vox*, January 18, 2017, https://www.vox .com/2017/1/18/14296126/white-segregated-suburb -neighborhood-cartoon.

12. Lloyd Wake, unpublished statement about Glide Celebrations, 1975, Glide archives.

## Chapter 5: Unity Is Not Uniformity

1. "The Character of a Methodist" (1739), in vol. 4 of *The Works of the Rev. John Wesley in Ten Volumes* (1826), 407.

2. *The Book of Discipline of The United Methodist Church 2016* (Nashville: United Methodist Publishing House, 2016), 57.

3. For more information about Affirmation, see http://www .umaffirm.org/site/. Another LGBTQ-affirming movement within The United Methodist Church is the Reconciling Congregations Program (www.rmnetwork.org). There are LGBTQ organizations in most denominations. To find one in your denomination, see https://www.huffingtonpost.com/2012/06 /24/gay-friendly-religious-communities_n_1616510.html or www.welcomingresources.org/links.htm.

## Chapter 6: We Eat with People We Love

1. "Wesley's Directions for Singing," Discipleship Ministries, The United Methodist Church, https://www.umcdiscipleship .org/resources/wesleys-directions-for-singing.

2. "By Water and the Spirit: A United Methodist Understanding of Baptism," http://www.umc.org/what-we-believe /by-water-and-the-spirit-a-united-methodist-understanding-of -baptism.

3. Ibid.

4. See www.rmnetwork.org for more information.

5. Members of LYNC included Affirmation (United Methodists for Lesbian, Gay, Bisexual, Transgender and Queer Concerns), Black Methodists for Church Renewal, Fossil Free UMC, MARCHA: Metodistas Asociados Representando la Causa Hispano-Americanos, Methodist Federation for Social Action (MFSA), Methodists in New Directions (MIND), National Federation of Asian American United Methodists (NFAAUM), Native American International Caucus (NAIC), Pacific Islanders Caucus of United Methodists (PINCUM), Reconciling Ministries Network, United Methodist Association of Ministers with Disabilities, and the Western Methodist Justice Movement (WMJM).

6. A video of the presentation is available at https://youtu.be /Bsmaon6rIdY.

7. According to its website, the Institute on Religion and Democracy is a "faith-based alliance of Christians who monitor, comment, and report on issues affecting the Church. We seek to reform the Church's role in public life, protect religious freedom, and support democracy at home and abroad. We are Christians working to reaffirm the church's biblical and historical teachings, strengthen and reform its role in public life, protect religious freedom, and renew democracy at home and abroad." With its conservative agenda, the IRD regularly attacks mainline Protestant denominations for their theological and social views. The IRD has as its vision an effort to "lead the fight rallying Christians to champion biblical, historic Christianity and its role in democratic society, and to defeat revisionist challenges." See https://theird.org for more information.

8. Henri J. M. Nouwen, *With Open Hands* (Notre Dame, IN: Ave Maria Press, 2006), 92.

CPSIA information can be obtained
at www.ICGtesting.com
Printed in the USA
FSHW01n0222250718
50808FS

9 780664 263607